Men Are From Penis!

by

Phil Cook

Bloomington, IN
authorHOUSE®
Milton Keynes, UK

AuthorHouse™
1663 Liberty Drive, Suite 200
Bloomington, IN 47403
www.authorhouse.com
Phone: 1-800-839-8640

AuthorHouse™ UK Ltd.
500 Avebury Boulevard
Central Milton Keynes, MK9 2BE
www.authorhouse.co.uk
Phone: 08001974150

This book is a work of non-fiction. Unless otherwise noted, the author and the publisher make no explicit guarantees as to the accuracy of the information contained in this book and in some

First published by AuthorHouse 2/6/2007

ISBN: 978-1-4259-7310-0 (sc)

Printed in the United States of America
Bloomington, Indiana

This book is printed on acid-free paper.

TABLE OF CONTENTS

CHAPTER 1: WHAT PLANET ARE YOU FROM?

"Imagine that men are from Mars and women are from Venus. One day long ago, the Martians, looking through their telescopes, discovered the Venusians. Just glimpsing the Venusians awakened feelings they had never known. They fell in love and quickly invented space travel and flew to Venus. The Venusians welcomed the Martians with open arms. They had intuitively known that this day would come. Their hearts opened wide to a love they had never felt before. The love between the Venusians and Martians was magical. They delighted in being together, doing things together and sharing together. Though from different worlds, they revelled in their differences. They spent months learning about each other, exploring and appreciating their different needs, preferences and behaviour patterns. For years, they lived together in love and harmony. Then they decided to fly to Earth. In the beginning, everything was wonderful and beautiful. But the effects of Earth's atmosphere took hold, and one morning everyone woke up with a peculiar kind of amnesia - selective amnesia! Both the Martians and Venusians forgot they were

from different planets and were supposed to be different. In one morning, everything they had learned about their differences was erased from their memory. And since that day, men and women have been in conflict".
(John Gray 'MEN ARE FROM MARS, WOMEN ARE FROM VENUS')

Women are from Venus and men are from Mars. Mmmm. So, the fairer sex come from the distant star named after the Roman goddess of love. And us geezers - we are direct descendants of a chocolate confection of astronomical proportions (astronomical - see what I did there?). Although this hackneyed statement regarding our origins has now become part of the vernacular in this multilingual language we call English, these actual comparisons between the sexes was only raised as recently as 1992, by one John Gray. A pseudonym for a sex-starved female novelist methinks. Wrong. At the time of writing, Mr Gray was a fully-functional Mars-tian with a wife & 3 daughters and whatever one may think of his/her opinions, the fact that he had procreated on at least 3 occasions and was still resident at the breakfast table, goes some way to endorsing his theories on "understanding the communication styles between men and women". So, after years of evolution and at a time when the sexes are considered to be equals, why do we still consider ourselves to be so far removed from our opposite gender? It's one of the great mysteries of life, on a par with: Do Eskimos put ice in their drinks and whatever happened to white dog poo? By the end of this book, all of these riddles may well have been solved and I can return to my mundane existence, happy in the knowledge that I've enlightened the lives of others.

VENUS: *One of the inferior planets and the second nearest to the sun, visible as a bright morning or evening star. It's surface is extremely hot (over 400 degrees cent) and is completely shrouded by dense cloud. The atmosphere is principally carbon dioxide. Mean distance from sun: 108 million km; period of revolution around sun: 225 days; period of axial rotation: 244.3 days (retrograde motion); diameter and mass: 96.5 and 81.5% that of earth respectively.*

MARS: The 4th planet from the sun, having a reddish-brown surface with numerous dark patches and 2 white polar caps. It has a thin atmosphere, mainly carbon dioxide, and low surface temperatures. Spacecraft encounters have revealed a history of volcanic activity and running surface water. The planet has 2 tiny satellites, Phobos and Delmos. Mean distance from sun: 228 million km; period of revolution around sun: 686.98 days; period of axial rotation: 24.6225 hours; diameter and mass: 53.2 and 10.7% that of earth respectively.

On Planet Earth in 2006, women are desirable, enigmatic, ambitious, sexy and - let's face it boys - as downright unfathomable as ever. Some guys feel they understand their opposite number and for the past 20yrs or so, at a time when I was co-habitating/going steady/married/in love/banging away like a window in an episode of 'Scooby Doo' (if you want to play the game, delete as necessary), this is exactly how I felt. Of course you understand them - they are a constant presence. We take it for granted that we know what makes them tick because if we didn't, they wouldn't be there - right? And when they're not there (and as you've probably gathered from my being alone with my computer, '*they' certainly are not), that is when the doubts creep in as to our perceptions of the female psyche. Maybe 'we' take women for granted or maybe 'they' don't understand the complexities of our larger brain capacity (think Homer, not Homer Simpson). Maybe our evolution process still hasn't evolved sufficiently for one half of the population to understand the other, or maybe we really are still 120 million kilometres apart, as highlighted above.

(If any astronomers, physicists, scientific boffins etc are reading this, please don't write to the publishers emphasising the inaccuracy of my data. I'm sure that once you take into consideration the rotation of the planets, gravitational pull, blah blah etc, the proximity between Venus and Mars is probably less or greater than 120 million km. But we don't care. And it's a well-known fact that scientists, along with traffic wardens and Elvis impersonators, never get sex anyway. If they do, they don't deserve it).

Of course, this should be a two-way argument although as you've probably read from the previous paragraph, this book is already lurching towards a male-orientated spin. The 2 main reasons behind this are as follows: 1) I'm a geezer. 2) Men are entirely more straight-forward than girlies - generally sweatier, less reliable, hairier, less romantic and more belligerent - but far more straight-forward. Let's look at some hard facts:-

Venus is an 'inferior' planet. From this snippet of information, one can only deduce that us Mars-tians are from a superior place. Venus is extremely hot whilst their distant neighbours are oh-so-much

cooler. Dude. Venus is 'dense', it has a greater diameter and mass (achieved in it's mid-30's after childbirth) and unlike the Planet Mars, there has never been any sign of life. Godammit, my home (it's getting personal now) even has 2 satellites named after characters from 'Only Fools and Horses'.

So yes, women <u>are</u> from Venus and men <u>are</u> from Mars.

(If any Venusians are still reading, please note that the aforementioned statement is said tongue-in-cheek and by the end of this book, you will indeed be wishing to replicate this action. Your tongue, my cheek).

But my purpose in life isn't to re-emphasise the findings of Mr Gray. What I intend to do is help build that spaceship that takes 21st-century Mars-tians to the promised land, if they really want to go there. Reverse thrust is an obvious pre-requisite specification, as is a La-z-Boy chair. But do you Mars-tians really want to make the journey or are you happy to continue participating in our 'War Of The Worlds', knowing that - without somebody taking the lead - future civilisations may struggle to co-exist on this neutral planet?

On July 21st 1969, Neil Armstrong became the first man to walk on the moon. The term 'first' is very much irrelevant, as nobody else has barely ever bothered to follow suit (6 moon landings all told). Many years before, somewhere in Asia, somebody decided to take the penis of a tiger, boil it in a soup and drink it to aid their own virility. Eons ago, somewhere in Darkest Africa, somebody decided to skewer their cheeks (facial, not anal) with long, sharpened slivers of wood to ward off evil spirits....and angry tigers, relieved of their genitalia.

Despite the absurdities of their actions, these folks were pioneers because their actions have been replicated by their own peoples. But the moon, 384,400 kilometres from Earth and the only other satellite accessible to Earthlings, remains free of dome-headed, bouncing visitors, which is good news for the millions of people who don't live there. The irony of it all is that President John F Kennedy signed up to the Apollo space project in 1961, at a time when the Russians - with the first space satellite and the first man to orbit the Earth - seemed far ahead in the space race. When the 11th Apollo mission successfully landed on the moon, 8yrs, several lives and millions of dollars had elapsed. Then, in their wisdom, the Mars-tians announced "That's it. Been there, done that, worn the t-shirt. No point in going back". And there-in lies the problem. We know women are from Venus, a distant land where love is the key but where too many other vagaries cloud any hope of an eternal, happy, harmonic co-existence. Women know we are from Mars, a distant land named after the god of war where what you see is what you get, no matter how sweaty, hairy or belligerent it may be. The Venusians love us - or humour us - because no matter how alien we are, they have accepted us for who we are. The fact that they haven't acquired the necessary skills to build their own spaceship and search the galaxy for more intelligent life-forms (which must surely exist), obviously has nowt to do with it! But whilst us lads have travelled from our distant land and adapted accordingly to life on Earth and the strange customs that it brings, have we really persevered with understanding the intricacies of our opposite species? Or does Mars bar that (Mars Bar - see what I did there?)? As Mr Gray stated, having touched-down on Earth, we all lived in unison and enjoyed learning about each other's backgrounds. Our ancestors and the African continent - as I will discuss later in the book - are a prime example of this. But I fear that for most of the 3 billion testosterone-driven boys/lads/men/geezers/gentlemen on this planet, there is a danger that the Earth's atmosphere has indeed taken it's toll and we're in danger of flying back to Mars, where we will proceed to point our lenses at some other planet, such as Jupiter. Though we'll need a frigging big telescope to do so.

So, I have taken it upon myself to share my knowledge in the hope of saving future man/woman kind. I feel I am qualified to do so because like John Gray Ph.D, I too have letters after my name although mine are an anagram of WANERK. I have always been a loving, domesticated, patient soul who has taken the time to understand women and their many foibles. I have loved and been loved. I have made love to many beautiful women. OK, that was a lie. But now, at the age of 42, I'm single for the first time since my teens and celibacy is now an integral, though somewhat unwelcome, part of my life. And now, I realise, that yes - we are so different. In my unerring quest for solutions, I will endeavour to undertake more research, particularly if it gives me the opportunity to extract the saliva's of an opposite being. And for the record, I have never been happy being compared to a sweet, sickly chocolate bar. I prefer fudge - one likes to have a finger every day.

*Footnote: In this context, 'they' means any one member of the female gender. This doesn't imply that I have, at any time in my life, indulged in a threesome or anything else of that ilk. But at this stage, my research is in it's infancy.

TAKE ON BOARD - When undertaking your journey, this book is an essential travel companion. You may not benefit from its contents but pretending to read it will stop the ignoramus in the adjacent seat from talking to you.

CHAPTER 2: GET LOST!

Profile for Gypsy 396.
Their chat-up line:- *"maybe one day i will understand how the mind works of the male population!!!!!"*
Location: Tamworth
In their own words:
"I hate this part, Im looking for a friendship to start with and then well who knows what the future holds for any of us. Im very honest probably to honest for my own good, but thats me. Kind considerate, reliable, trustworthy, domesticated. But not a fool and dont let anybody walk all over me. Ive been hurt to many times and now I've learned my lesson. I do av a sense of humour, but i am also shy at first then once i'm relaxed with someone then i come out of my shell i apologise for the pic as it was taken on a very stressful day as i had just received some bad news and i keep forgetting batteries for camera to take some more sorry. I like to wear jeans most of the time, but i do also like to dress up for going out, although i've never had the opportunity to wear a ball gown, i wouldn't mind trying it though lol. Im currently attending college

studying access course and hopefully October 2006 will be going to university to study either radiography or physiotherapy, not sure which one yet. so if there are any potential patients out there for me get in touch. I enjoy cooking and i can make a wicked indian curry. My favourite films are four weddings and a funeral, gladiator, armageddon (only because of Ben Affleck) lol. Shrek 2 any chick flick films. Music erm: ub40, celine dion, blue, scissor sisters, bon jovi, phil collins and eighties. I dont like one stands they r so cold, im looking for a relationship with someone i can fall in love with and trust as i was married for 12 years and the whole time i was being cheated on, i am not gonna go through that again. I am independent but it would be nice to av someone i can as for advice especially about bloody cars (like when my tyres need replacing i got pulled over by the police but they let me off) im replacing them now. Also i love to play pool and quite good at it as well. Also i dont like mind games so dont try em i also dont like weirdo's either I can sus em straight away. As u can by the pic ive tried scuba diving a couple of years ago in fuerterventura. I will try anything once within reason of course lol." (JULY 2005)

The journey our male ancestors (as from this moment on, they will no longer be referred to as Mars-tians as you can only take a joke so far) took was hazardous & long and what we now have to determine is how our 21st Century descendants can bring it on themselves to make a shorter, but equally ground-breaking expedition. It's time to reach out and touch tentacles. Travelling across space, those early pioneers would have had to make a refuelling pit-stop on a then barren Earth, which - at that stage - was totally devoid of the female form as we know it. Somewhere like Reading. But the journey had to be undertaken and the Marstians (sorry) were on a mission. Having spied on the Venusians with their high-powered telescopic lenses, they were determined to meet these voluptuous creatures and have....SEX! For years, the superior race had observed their not-so-near neighbours with one hand firmly wrapped around their implement - tripods weren't available on Mars. They had sustained a wonderful sense of arousal, a feeling heightened by strange gravitational forces that only mid-space can bring. But as we have found to our cost ever since, sex is OK but you can't beat the real thing. Heck, how do you think 'Hands Solo' got his name!? Even his nemesis Darth Vader perfected his trademark heavy breathing by spending hours watching the Venusians from a distant galaxy, far, far away.....

Over a 50yr period from the end of the 19th Century onwards, the British became entwined in 3 major wars. Virtually the entire world were either instigators of colonialism or on the receiving end of repression and apartheid. The world was expanding but shrinking too, as the 'super-powers' attempted to gain further footholds in countries other than their own and oppression, racial bigotry & rebellion rose their ugly heads around the globe. But for the purpose of this study, we will ignore the rest of the world because whilst interactions between English-speaking Venusians and their uglier peers have deteriorated during the latter part of the last century and up to the present day, most other nations have managed to sustain relationships to the extent where full blown civil war is unlikely rather than imminent. Throughout these dark days, our grandparents & great-grandparents had to endure food rationing, general strikes, power cuts, illness, high mortality rates, unemployment and extreme poverty. Life was tough but less was more. Men and women worked harder together to understand each-others needs and despite their vastly different DNA, the alien life-forms lived happily together on Planet Earth and endured all that could be thrown at them. They communicated. This was an age before computers, Dyson's, Micro-Noodles, disposable condoms, iPod's and Dale Winton. But they were happy. Of course, in the late 19th Century/early 20th Century, the role of women in society was vastly different to that of today. Equality wasn't part of the English, Venusian or Marstian dialect and women could only dream about the role in society that they quite rightly hold today. But things weren't oh-so-different. In 1902, women were permitted to study for a degree qualification for the first time ever, despite having been allowed to attend centres of higher education for a number of years. On December 28th 1918, women turned out to exercise their right to vote for the first time although at that stage, only property-owners over the age of 30 were eligible. In that same year, a Scottish-Venusian named Marie Stopes published 2 books that caused an immediate furore. The first, 'Married Love', openly discussed sexual relationships from a female perspective and the second, 'Wise Parenthood', advocated sex education and birth control for women. So, Earth was evolving and having had a planet entirely to themselves, Venusians wanted at least a 50-50 share in their new home, with equal rights too. But our grandparents accepted these changes and communication was still as prevalent as ever. So what has happened since? Are Marstians unable to reach out to Venusians because their evolution has meant they are no longer those innocent, vulnerable, beings that were discovered many moons ago? If Benny Andersson had been christened Roger, would he have called his group A BRA rather that ABBA? Questions, questions? But whilst our grandparents are prime examples of how the 2 alien life-forms can still communicate despite an ever-changing world, notice how they never sit together. Old peeps love their own chair. Try this experiment in the comfort of your own home - invite nanny & gramps round for tea, then proceed to sit on all of the single chairs. It's well-known that the old and infirm can not sit together on a settee. If gran sits down on the sofa, grandad will probably stand by the fireplace, warming his catheter against an imaginary log fire. If he grabs the seat first, granny will insist on helping in the kitchen. It's a great game - try it.

What do you call a woman who's lying on the bed, struggling to do up her size 12 jeans?

Answer: A Venusian fly-trap.

Guys. Picture Great Britain as a feminine form, sitting and looking forlornly towards the Irish Sea. Her long legs sweep seductively from Lands End to the East and Home Counties. Not surprisingly, due to the uncomfortable nature of the pose, she suffers from Penzance Needles (I'm doing my best here!). East-Anglia acts as her over-generous rump, protruding into the North Sea. As her back arches upwards from The Wash to the North-West coast of England, her torso stretches from the North Midlands to North Yorkshire. Scotland constitutes her pretty head and with the Solway Firth appearing to be her gob, Barrow acts as a huge zit on her chin. As for Wales, for the purpose of this vague analysis, we'll just say that she's pregnant. Now, where d'ya wanna go? Well, most of us have been to London and if we haven't, that's the happening place to go. Why London? Well, it's conveniently situated at the top of her legs and if you endeavour to get right in there and double-back on yourself, you will find Gatwick, otherwise known as the G-Spot. But Marstians don't like asking directions and are more than likely going to get lost. Now, if your loved one asks you to travel to Scotland, the sweaty, hairy, belligerent reply is likely to go something along the lines of "but they've only got 2 football teams, the men wear skirts, the cows have horns and the weather is always pants". Which, of course, is entirely true. But once the Marstian race endeavour to make that journey into the unknown - and if you haven't caught up yet, Scotland represents the mind and engine room of our beloved - they will discover a land of plenty. OK, there's a lot of wilderness up there known as The Highlands but there is so much more going on too. *You will want to return again & again and the more you go back, the more you will learn. We spent years building a spaceship in order to meet new civilisations, so why not take the time to make that short journey up North. We know the South is warmer & more welcoming and we know that the South Midlands is a waste. OK, it's actually the waist but any spare flesh between the breasts (Liverpool/Manchester area) and the female genitalia (London) can only really be described as a waste. And don't be afraid to ask the way.

*Footnote: Please note that I have not, at any stage, received any form of payment from the Scottish Tourist

Board for endorsing their fab country. Nothing was sent in a jiffy bag to my home in - according to the above map - the bellybutton.

They are looking for:

"Im looking for someone whos the same really honest as i hate lies, trustworthy, etc. Knows how to treat a lady. Someone who is willing to start off with a freindship and then to progress into much more as i believe a partner should be a best friend and soulmate. Id prefer a non smoker as i dont smoke, who drinks occasionally, hes gotta have a good personality and a wicked sense of humour. looks well i think its wots inside that matters, to a certain extent anyway. Needs to be down to earth, who i feel totally relaxed and comfortable with, needs to be a good listener and a romantic as i am also a romantic. Also must like children as i have three and they r my life and we come as a package. i'd prefer a guy whos of stocky build a bit of meat on him, and muscle, short dark hair dresses trendy no old fogies"

TAKE ON BOARD - A map. Quite simply, Marstians are useless at finding their way to places they are not familiar with. Mine's a large one.

CHAPTER 3: LET'S GET CONNECTED.

April 8th hasn't exactly been a benchmark for life-changing historical events over the years. For the record, it was on this date in 1917 that Panama declared war on Germany. Cosmic. Their contribution to the end of World War I has long since been consigned to the history books - well, in Panama anyway. On April 8th 1973, Spanish painter Pablo Picasso curled his toes for the final time and exactly 21yrs later, cult-hero Kurt Cobain guaranteed himself immortality by blowing his brains out at his Seattle home. But for me, April 8th 2005 will always be a day when my life changed, for better for worse. This was the day that I logged on to my computer and unleashed the monster that is ...on-line dating.

It is patently obvious that different peeps have different reasons and motives for registering with on-line dating agencies, telling lies about themselves and then talking to total strangers. Of course, one shouldn't make sweeping statements such as that but there are 2 main reasons why I will stand my ground on this: 1) I've never been intimate enough with anybody offering 'electronic hugs' to find out whether they really are who they claim to be. But my research shows that many people who have made that big step and have actually met the person on the other end of their mouse, have discovered that they were not all they claimed to be. 2) It's my book.

In a world where communication and interaction between the species has become more fraught than ever, talking to someone without actually talking has become the chosen weapon of the masses. Whether you've cheated on your wife, stabbed your husband, love line-dancing, look like Ann Widdecombe or are just generally one of life's losers, there is nothing stopping you from sharing juices across the internet. Ugliness doesn't help of course and it pays to find a camera that <u>does</u> lie, portraying you as Brad Pitt rather than Cess Pit. One of my friends is so ugly that when he went speed-dating recently, all of the girls put their watches forward. I digress. Talking about on-line dating should actually be Chapter 4 and communication in general was to be covered in Chapter 3 but I'm so concerned for the welfare of mankind, I think the boys from the Red Planet should know sooner rather than later, exactly what they are dealing with.

(The following paragraph is deadly serious and personal so I would appreciate it if you could imagine a symphony of melancholy music whilst reading it.)

I decided to take a peak at on-line dating after a traumatic start to my year. In the February, I had suffered a painful - although almost inevitable - split from my girlfriend. At the age of 41, I should've be big enough and ugly enough to absorb it but for the first time in my life, I was truly hurt. Here was somebody I had loved dearly and who had entered my world 2yrs previous, at a time when I needed something special. I never stopped telling her that I loved her. We shared many things together and had so much in common. When I couldn't be with her, I sent her ditties and poetry to show that although I wasn't there, I WAS with her. When she cried, I kissed away her tears. I constantly tried to surprise her and make her laugh. Eventually, I sacrificed almost everything in a vain attempt to make our relationship work. In return, I received an all-consuming love like I'd never felt before. But with it came a dark side. Unconditional love it certainly wasn't. My X was beset with anger, jealousy and demons from her past relationships and no matter how I tried to exorcise these demons with love, honesty and communication, eventually it was to destroy us. Like alcoholics and gamblers who refuse to accept they have a problem, she couldn't be cured because in the cold light of day, that dark side that had raised its ugly head suddenly didn't exist. It was my problem, not hers. Being single for the first time in 20yrs+ isn't a problem but when you find yourself with your nose pressed up against the outside of the bubble looking in, you beat yourself up about what else you could have done. We've all been there. Like the thousands of people whose profiles are posted on-line, I could be anyone. I could be lying. But I am, fundamentally, a nice, loving, honest guy. So you can imagine how I felt when I found my X had signed up to an on-line dating agency and had opened her profile with the words "Why do I always pick the bad 'uns....."

Take what you read with a large pinch of Saxo.

In this day and age, it is our divine right to remain cynical. But for the purpose of research and in a vain attempt to find somebody who shares my love of The Buzzcocks, pancakes and 'Bargain Hunt', I scoured the internet and have built a database of hard facts that all Marstians (stating that I wasn't going to use this terminology again as early as Chapter 2 was a stupid mistake/lie, although I hope the streamlined spelling aids your literary enjoyment) can now have access to.

Knowledge is a weapon and the following list is your very own light sabre!

10 THINGS YOU NEED TO KNOW ABOUT VENUSIANS.

1) Venusians lurrrrrve spontaneity but 9 out of 10 of them can't even spell it.
2) Venusians like to be tickled so a good sense of humour is a must.
3) Venusians have an unhealthy appetite for movies set in prisons.
4) Although "looks aren't important", Venusians still want tall, dark and handsome.
5) Venusians are all, quintessentially, water babes.
6) Venusians tend to underestimate their size, so if they say they're large - beware!
7) All Venusians are impatient - as if you didn't know that already!
8) Words are important but for a good way to break the ice, Venusians love poetry.
9) The previous 8 statements are true. The next one isn't.
10) 71% of all Venusians have lesbian tendencies.

1. SPONTANEITY: *1. the state or quality of being spontaneous. 2. the exhibiting of actions, impulses, or behaviour that are stimulated by internal processes.*

Spontaniety, spontanity, sponteneity - if you go on-line, you'll see it all. But what is it about impulsive actions that stimulates Venusians so? Of course, not all types of spontaneity are welcome. An impromtu slap round the face or an unprovoked tirade or assault are all spontaneous actions and as for 'spontaneous combustion', that can leave quite a nasty singe on your shag-pile. What girlies love is a nice surprise. It may be romantic, rewarding, unexpected but at the end of the day, it has to be a gesture that comes - without prompting - from the heart or the wallet. The older we get, the more difficult it is to deliver those spontaneous moments because of work, family and quite often or not, financial restraints. But the older they get (by referring to Venusians as 'they', I am withdrawing my tentacle and am in danger of referring to the opposite sex as a 3rd party, like the majority of Marstians), the more they expect us to be impulsive. A kiss, flowers, going out with them, going down on them - we know what women like but don't do it too often, otherwise they'll expect it every day. And that's not spontaneous. Finally, try this out. When she sits down to watch 'East-bloody-Enders' on the Beeb, tell her you're off down the pub. That IS spontaneous!

2. A GOOD S.O.H: Its often been said that a woman can be 'laughed into bed'. Nice theory, but can you imagine Ken Dodd & Jo Brand getting more sex because of their chosen professions? I think not. But it's certainly true that women like a good titter and there's no better titters

than us Marstians. Making the Venusians laugh shouldn't be too difficult because we are such an absurd bunch of space-travellers, we have a Pandora's box (do girls called Pandora really exist?) positively brimming with humorous material. Self-deprecation is absolutely essential. Before laughing at others, make sure you can extract the urine from yourself. Being a figure of parody and taking the p**s out of yourself not only gives the lady in your life a feeling of reassurance, it also takes away one of her most annoying traits - taking the p**s outta us! But there's a time and place for humour and if she does burst into laughter every time you drop your boxers in the bedroom, tell her she's very funny.....and reminds you of Jo Brand!!

If meeting somebody in a pub/club/supermarket/salsa class/police station (delete as necessary) for the first time, you could always try and make an instant impression by making them laugh. For instance: What's 60ft long and smells of piss? Answer: A conga in an old folks' home! No? Then try telling 'em something absurdly funny that they couldn't possibly know, like: "Did you know that 'You Like Minge' is an anagram of Kylie Minogue?" Then again, perhaps not.

3. PRISON MOVIES: Difficult to understand why Venusians have such a penchant for the films 'The Shawshank Redemption' & 'The Green Mile'. Released in 1994, 'Shawshank' wasn't a big box office hit and it wasn't until its release onto DVD, did its popularity soar and it's now regarded as one of the Top 5 most popular films of all time. Likewise, 'The Green Mile' didn't exactly set the box office on fire. Being based on a Stephen King novel and with Tom Hanks in the lead, it was a vastly

more marketable product but at more than 3hrs long, the general public generally stayed away. So, what's the secret? Well, I dunno. Quintessentially, the films are feel-good movies despite being set in a violent and intimidating environment. Both of the main leads turn out to be good souls, innocent of the crimes for which they've been incarcerated. And both films are pretty much devoid of romance, though there is plenty of male-bonding. Maybe it's the fight against the odds that moistens the lips of the fairer sex. But my exhaustive research has uncovered something much simpler, much more sinister and far more plausible than that. It's all about men in uniforms.

4. T, D & H: "Looks aren't important, it's what inside that counts but I do like 'em tall, dark and handsome". Yawn. Sorry, just dropping off there. Isn't it amazing that after light years spent alone on Planet Venus where the occupants spent their days pruning their bushes, watching the Sun reflect off of telescopic lenses miles away and waiting for somebody to invent 'Celebrity Love Island', Venusians now have the cheek to demand exactly what type of Mars-tian they want. Of course, looks aren't everything but given the choice, all of us would rather be with someone whom it is safe to kiss goodnight with the lights still on. I will talk about meeting, greeting and sleeping with the not-so-attractives later in the book. Tall, dark and handsome is very European, very sultry and very mysterious. Women don't want someone who's fightable, they want a bloke who can fight a bull. So, be as European as poss. Dye your hair black, show off as much body hair as possible, smile enigmatically, talk in a foreign language, carve a big letter Z onto her pillowcase before making love

and if making her a spontaneous meal (don't forget, this has to be spontaneous but if it overrides the fact that you are short, ginger and ugly and it works, forget what was said in No:2), make sure it's a pizza.

5. WATER BABES: It's highly surprising to find that Venusians love water. On the planet they called home for so long, water doesn't exist. But on Planet Earth, they can't get enough of the stuff, whether it's skiing, scuba diving, swimming or just lying on a beach. Women love to be near the sea and the hotter the weather, the more their thirst for the wet stuff accelerates. Living on Venus so near to the sun, led its occupants to wishing for companionship from afar. It is well known that extremes of weather can seriously slow down the metabolism and hinder rational thought. So, take the old girl on holiday to Egypt and their Venusian mind, which has evolved far quicker than the Marstian one, should return to being on a par with ours.

6. SIZE OF A WOMAN: One of the most scariest things about on-line dating is looking at the pictures. Yes, I know, I'm hardly an Adonis myself but what I did do was to describe myself accurately - 5ft8/9inches (sorry, 42yr-olds don't do metric), medium build and kind of cute. But some of the descriptions both sexes may encounter actually belie the accompanying photograph. A large proportion of women - and the older they are, the larger the proportions - don't actually upload a snapshot of themselves onto their profile. This is worrying. The old adage 'if you've got it, flaunt it' must be taken seriously because if you have, you do. Maybe they couldn't fit their massive girth into the

photo-booth at Boots or maybe there's a more innocent, plausible excuse. But beware. To help you on-line virgins, here is a rough translation of Venusian language when it comes to talking about size:-

- *ATHLETIC: Usually means fit and healthy and is an accurate description*
- *SLIM: Generally an honest description although 'slim' can vary between languages*
- *MEDIUM: Means they've had too many pies - A Bit Overweight*
- *A BIT OVERWEIGHT: Means their lips should be stapled together - Large*
- *LARGE: Accurate description, only because huge isn't an option. Coach parties welcome*

7. IMPATIENCE: Nothing new here. But Venusians don't deny it. On the average profile, they will put Fidelity, Fitness and just about any other category as more important than Patience. And when you see just how many women fail to complete their profiles, the evidence is there for all to see. Case closed.

8. POETRY: There are many things that the fairer sex love to indulge themselves in. Some of the many examples of leisure activities seen listed on dating agencies include walking, shoes, music, wakeboarding, horror films, aerobics, animals, chick flicks, dancing, horse riding, gigging, swimming, crochet, soap operas, reading, mountain-biking, line-dancing, eating, scuba diving and the list goes on and on. Poetry is a notable absentee. But Venusians love words of wit & wisdom and being lovers of

romance & humour, the lead in your pencil could yet aid the lead in your pencil. Of all of the ladies I contacted online for the purposes of research and pervish gratification, only about 20% responded in any way and most of them enjoyed overusing the word "off". But the response from ladies to whom I sent ditties was about 56% and would've have been higher if it wasn't for my face. Then again, 99% of all surveys are bollocks!

9. Everything you have read in this chapter is true, except for the fact that I'm <u>exceptionally</u> cute.

10. 72% is probably nearer the mark but I'm saving lesbians for later.

TAKE ON BOARD: A pair of handcuffs. It's a prison thing and though it may not turn your home into a Shawshank, it may make your bedroom into a sure shag.

CHAPTER 4: U TALKING 2 ME?

COMMUNICATION: 1. the act or an instance of communicating; the impairing or exchange of information, ideas or feelings

As John Gray highlights in *'Men Are From Mars, Women Are From Venus'*, when the two species first made contact, the spoken word was not an option, as neither could speak t'others language. But once we'd all touched down on Planet Earth and commenced to live as one, a new universal language was to be born. As a cacophony of sound and signals developed, the English language - as we know it - came into being (the term 'came into being' can also be used if Marstians have sex with the type of Venusian described in Casebook 1:Chapter 5). At this stage, the sounds were positive, inquisitive, loving. Terms like "And what time do you think this is?", "What you staring at?", "Not tonight, I'm got a headache" and "No Gran, I don't care if your hip replacement is starting to buckle, get back in that f***ing kitchen" were unheard of and it's only in the latter part of the 20th Century, that such barbs threatened to tear this language apart.

"When the Martians and Venusians first got together, they encountered many of the problems with relationships we have today. Because they recognised that they were different, they were able to solve these problems. One of the secrets of their success was good communication. Ironically, they communicated well because they spoke different languages. When they had problems, they would just go to a translator for assistance. Everyone knew that people from Mars and people from Venus spoke different languages, so when there was a conflict, they didn't start judging or fighting but instead pulled out their phrase dictionaries to understand each other more fully. If that didn't work, they went to a translator for help".

(John Gray 'MEN ARE FROM MARS, WOMEN ARE FROM VENUS')

So, where have we (or should I say YOU) gone wrong? Why, having developed bigger, more complex satellite systems that have globalised an already efficient two-way communication process, are we unable to understand her/him indoors? Well, as the 2 species have evolved over the years, the 50/50 equality ratio has now become unbalanced. The so-called 'weaker sex' are stronger academically and tend to mature at a much faster rate. Although most of the great inventions and groundbreaking achievements that moulded the 20th Century were created by ageing Marstians, it's the Venusians who have coped better with the changes that they brought. As time has gone on, new forms of communication have been developed to aid our society but many of these have only served to make the basic form of communication - face-to-face oral - that much more difficult. From body language and smoke signals, we have evolved through the telephone, Morse Code and semaphore, right up to the modern-day delights of texting and the famous chav 1-fingered salute. I once received a text message from a girlfriend saying *"luv u X"*. So, I naturally replied. I wrote *"and I do u too X"*. Only, I didn't. Because the whole point of texting is to abbreviate the words you want to say and not having the nous to understand such a language, only emphasises your total lack of street-cred (lol). Abbreviate and drop the vowels I was told. So, I replied with my heartfelt message that <u>actually</u> read *"& d 2 X"*. As the survivors of the Titanic said, you catch my drift? The mobile telephone has long since been taken for granted in the Western World but there is a worrying trend - the industries fastest growing market is in Africa. The poorest continent on the planet where, despite massive Third World debt, famine, civil war, trade embargos, extremes of weather, poverty and the vile curse that is Aids, the Marstians and Venusians still manage to co-exist in relative harmony. Yes, civil war has torn the heart out of this magnificent land and even in the peaceful African nations, there are still vast gulfs regarding different clans and religions but this is man v man. Not man v woman. So, at a time when the Africans need as much help as ever (it was recently been recorded that Africa is now officially poorer than ever), we are sending them mobile phones. Mmm. The Africans are a proud nation of traditions. Strong family values and the Marstians/Venusians ability to live in harmony is the backbone of this continent. Much of this land has largely been untouched by the 20th/21st Centuries and the horrors our contemporary society have brought. But what we must remember is that the reason African couples co-exist as they do, is largely because they don't have the modern day distractions and corporate greed that has so blighted the rest of the world. It is a lack of evolution - technologically and psychologically - that has kept the Third World Venusians and Mars-tians together.

"Jeremiah, you're gazelle is on the table - Table Mountain (lol)"

The female perception of love and the male equivalent are generally regarded to be vastly different. But make no bones about it, both men and women know how to love and be loved. But for women, it comes as an entity, an all-encompassing bubble of passion and emotion that they long to be within. Having learnt the art of reading, Venusians soon submerged themselves in 'Mills and Boon' and novels written by a batty old woman dressed in pink. If they weren't in love, they wanted to read about peeps who were. But for the male gender, it's different. On Planet Earth, Marstians took time to understand the beings from Planet Venus and they enjoyed experiencing a previously untapped wealth of inner warmth. But over a period of time, their priorities changed. They were to become hunter-gatherers, pioneers and warriors. And having stepped further and further outside the aforementioned bubble, the 21st Century Marstian now has difficulty getting back in. But when they do, the whole world knows about it. Most of the greatest love stories and songs of all time have been penned by the bearded ones. But it's the songs that really stand out. Whereas the female singer/songwriters continue to warble about luuurrvvvve, male singer/songwriters write about something more specific - an actual person. How many songs can you think of that are named after women? Well, there's loads. And although it's easy to pluck any name out of the air and put it in a song, it shows that for geezers, it is easier to identify love as a time, a place, a person - rather than just a generalism. Two of the biggest selling singles of all time were written in tribute to the writer's better-half - 'The Lady in Red' by Chris de Burgh and 'Uptown Girl' by Billy Joel (unless you are one of our younger readers, in which case it's by Westlife). As for the name game, it is probably far easier to get the important aspects of a relationship to rhyme with a girls name than vice-versa: Eg - Mandy/randy, Mary/hairy, Betty/sweaty, Heather/gusset. Sorry, that doesn't rhyme but I like the word 'gusset'. OK, the proof is in the pudding. Here are my Top 20 hit's with their highest chart position in brackets.

1. MANDY - Barry Manilow/Westlife (1)
2. ELOISE - Barry Ryan/The Damned (2)
3. JOANNA - Kool and the Gang (2)
4. KAYLEIGH - Marillion (2)
5. LOLA - The Kinks (2)
6. EMMA - Hot Chocolate (3)
7. NIKITA - Elton John (3)
8. ANGIE - The Rolling Stones (5)
9. CAROLINE - Status Quo (5)
10. GAYE - Clifford T.Ward (8)
11. SHERRY - The Four Seasons (8)
12. ROSETTA - Alan Price & Georgie Fame (11)
13. LAURA - Scissor Sisters (12)
14. ROSANNA - Toto (12)
15. ROXANNE - The Police (12)
16. LOUISE - The Human League (13)

17. MARY - Scissor Sisters (14)
18. CANDY - Ash (20)
19. LORRAINE - Bad Manners (21)
20. BERNADETTE - The Four Tops (23)

There are many more song titles named after women that I've long since forgotten and several other titles just lurking outside the Top 20 include 'Diane', 'Veronica' and probably the best one of all - 'Sarah' by Thin Lizzy which surprisingly, only reached No:24. Songs such as 'Oh Carol', 'Lady Lynda' & 'My Sharona' weren't considered otherwise Chapter 4 would have taken on an air of tedium. Of course, on closer scrutiny, huge rifts appear in my argument. Song No:15 was sung about a prostitute and at least 3 of the list (No's:7,13 & 17) were sung by Marstians batting for the Venusian side. George Michael wasn't omitted for this reason but when he sung about 'Faith', the feminine form was probably the last thing on his mind. For the argument: How many songs sung by female artistes are about a specific guy (the songs 'Ben', 'Daniel' & 'Michael' were sung by geezers)? Against the argument, how many modern day songs are written about specific women, as most of the above list are at least 20yrs old? But can you really imagine modern day ditties such as 'Fifi Trixiebelle' or 'Ambrosian Moonbucket'? Likewise, our fore-fathers never wrote songs entitled 'Beryl', 'Hilda' or 'Doris', safe in the knowledge that one day in the not-too-distant future, somebody would invent far funkier names.

I will close this chapter with probably the finest set of lyrics ever written. OK, that's a bit opinionated but that's the joy of writing a book.

> *"Everybody knows that you love me baby,*
> *Everybody knows that you really do.*
> *Everybody knows that you've been faithful,*
> *give or take a night or two.*
> *Everybody knows you've been discreet but there*
> *were so many people you just had to*
> *meet - without your clothes.*
> *And Everybody knows"*
> *('Everybody Knows' - LEONARD COHEN)*

TAKE ON BOARD - A pair of walkie-talkies. A mobile phone without the option of texting is the safest form of communication.

CHAPTER 5: GET BACK INTO LINE.

"So your honour, the case for the defence is blatantly simple. My client, with the future of man/woman kind at stake and suffering with a severe case of odibil, set out on this quest purely so others should reap the benefits. At no stage did he lie to any ladies about whom he was and if he has caused any long-term psychological damage to the aforementioned people due to his unpleasant looks, this is entirely the fault of the women themselves. They asked him to take off the paper bag. I rest my case and I trust that the prosecution will demand no further questioning from my client".

"But you don't have a case. That is quite clearly a box-file. I know a box-file when I see one".

"No your honour, it's a figure of speech. When I said I rest my case, it was meant as a metaphor. It means that I've said all I have to say and that my client's innocence is so straight-forward, nothing else needed to be added".

"What's a bloody odibil?"

"Its a reverse form of libido sir, hence the name. Most males between the ages of 16-36 get a nut-sack swollen to the size of Mount Kilimanjaro when they go without sex for any

long period of time but when you get to my clients age, the process goes into reverse and can malfunction".

"And what's this SEX that you keep talking about........?"

"Oh forget it sir. He's as guilty as sin".

CASEBOOK NO:1:-

Having never gone on a blind date in my whole life, the thought of meeting somebody in a pub for the first time filled me with trepidation. I'm the most easy-going guy in the world and I'll chat to anybody, but what if she looks more like **the** 'Babe' rather than a babe and what do I do if her face fails to disguise her obvious disappointment when we meet. What do I do if she plays with the straw in her Bacardi Breezer whilst continually looking at her watch? Maybe that's a come on. Maybe I'm just out of touch. Maybe my research, writings and expert(!) opinion are all misguided and you've had to wait until Chapter 5 to realise this book is a waste of your time. How will I know? At this stage, we need to get the unpleasantness out of the way. If you do walk into a pub and meet a Venusian who has any of the following traits, you will need to make your escape sharpish - A) She's so big, you can't see the bar, B) She has severe scratching or puncture marks situated on her arms, C) She hasn't shaved, D) Her hair is tied back so tight, she looks Japanese but isn't, E) She's drinking pints of 'Bishops Nipple' or F) She <u>does</u> still have tentacles. Of course, for the purpose of this study, most of the above can apply to both sexes. Anyway, my first potential date came with a lady from Gloucester. For the uninitiated amongst you, if I live in the bellybutton of England (see Chapter 2), Gloucester is a bit of flaky skin that has unwelcomingly (is that a real word?) lodged itself nearby. She was a 40yr-old primary school teacher and as you've probably already gathered, by using the term, 'potential', I didn't actually bother meeting her. On close inspection, it transpired that her on-line profile wasn't entirely compatible with mine. For starters, there was no picture. And she hated kids. Also, she made it quite clear that she hated smoking. Well, when it comes to the deadly weed, I really can take it or leave it and if I met the woman of my dreams and she was a non-smoker....bingo. Kill two birds with one stone. But no, not Gloucester woman. She made it quite clear that all-smokers should be totally eradicated from Planet Earth and returned to their planets of origin, in which case I would be typing this on my lap-top on Mars. Oh - and she was 5ft tall. So, on the morning of our meet, I texted the Oompa-Loompa from down the road and made my excuses. The fact that my foot was in plaster after a recent operation was a good enough excuse but as blind panic set in, I would have probably broken my own legs to avoid this woman. I'm sure she was lovely. And still is. But I had to start again from scratch.

(When it comes to 'compatible profiles', never expect any of your opposite number to share exactly the same interests. But opposites attract and if there's a Venusian who loves bungee-jumping, breeding guinea-pigs and drinking absinthe - hopefully, not all at the same time - give her a whirl. Particularly if she looks like Kate Beckinsale).

CASEBOOK NO:2:-

About the same time as this was going on, I befriended a lass from Basingstoke in Hampshire. For the record,

Basingstoke is situated towards the top of the outstretched leg, just short of the thigh. I knew she was interested in me because by the time we approached our date with destiny, she had browsed my profile no fewer than 17 times. We communicated a lot over a period of several weeks and as we got to know more about each-other, we decided it may be a good idea to meet up. I told her about my life, my son, the beautiful town in which I live, my hopes and dreams, my aspiration to be a writer, my job in cinema management etc, etc. She told me that she made sandwiches for local businesses and enjoyed getting p***ed. That's not entirely fair because she was fun and interesting but this was hardly a 'meeting of minds'. But suddenly, something struck home. There was a pattern emerging. Like Gloucester woman, Basingstoke lass was 40. 40? What in heaven's name do I want to go out with a 40yr-old for? For starters, they look like..... well, 40yr-olds! Now, evolution is in danger of becoming an over-used verb in the context of this book but it's important to understand the term exactly. It means a gradual change. Having been in constant relationships for the previous couple of decades with Venusians of the same age, I never saw them age from day-to-day. Whenever I stepped off of the dating conveyor belt - which I did at the ages of 20, 25 & 39 - I immediately stepped straight back on again. To be honest, I barely lifted a millimetre of bunion (for the record, I do not have anything resembling a bunion but to emphasise the point, it has more projection than a verruca, a corn or athlete's foot) off of the production line because I had slight 'overlaps'. The Venusian term for this is 'double-dating' or 'having an affair'. Except for when they do it, in which case its called "don't worry about him, he's gay". The actual Latin term for this cross-over is *CONSISTENTUS EVENBETTERUS ERECTI.* So, as I was saying, on a day-to-day basis, you don't see your loved ones change. Our children grow daily but we don't see these changes ('we' being us fathers who share responsibilities, even after break-up/divorce etc). It's only when your ageing, confused old Uncle Frida comes to visit and says "My god, he/she's grown" that you realise - yes, he/she has. If I was still with my wife or my subsequent girlfriend, I would still love them for who they are and age wouldn't be an issue. But to meet someone new now, who has already lived through 40yrs+ without me.....and it shows? Mmmm, dunno. I decided against it and declined the offer of visiting an upper thigh. Though little did I know, I would be going there regardless...........

CASEBOOK NO:3:-

In May 2005, I finally plucked up the courage to meet somebody whom I had been talking to on-line. As was the case with No's 1 & 2, this particular female took an interest in me after I'd sent her an amusing ditty based upon her name. Although I would like to share these pieces of poetical genius with my readers, it would be unfair to do so at the risk of exposing the anonymity of the aforementioned ladies. Using prose as an ice-breaker has an extremely high success rate but like the Titanic, some times you can fail to cut the ice and sink without trace. Casebook No:3 probably didn't even understand the irony of my humour because she was Russian. Even more importantly, she was only 37. On my oh-so-accurate map of the female-form in Chapter 2, Russia doesn't exactly figure but luckily enough, she was a tad nearer to home.

She lived in Newbury. Now, whether you visit Newbury on my hypothetical map or in real-life, it's a pretty fine place to go. Unfortunately, we were to meet in a coffee bar in Reading. For some unearthly reason (and yes, we are all 'unearthly' but I am trying to talk from a down-to-earth perspective here), I decided to meet my new best friend wearing a t-shirt underneath a suit. Why? What possessed me? Having spent all of this time opening my heart and telling peeps who/what I am really am, here I was dressed in attire that was a contradiction in styles and a contradiction of the very person I claimed to be. Yes, I wear a lot of casual wear. Yes, I can look quite dapper in a suit. But no, I don't usually mix the two. It's akin to putting vodka on my Toad In The Hole or self-abusing whilst watching 'Top Gear'. Certain pleasures should not be confused and for the record, I do like Jeremy Clarkson. But not that much. Anyway, I amble into coffee bar - Amazonian woman looks up from table - she offers hand, I offer lips - pleasantries exchanged - she carries on munching her Black Forest Gateaux - end of story. She certainly didn't look like Anthea Turner as she had on her profile although if you imagine a larger, greyer version and squint a little, well yes, there's a definite likeness. Her English was poor and it was for that very reason I had initiated our meet, because she had difficulty communicating on-line. In person, things weren't a great deal better. After a pleasant, somewhat fractured hour together, we parted, agreeing never to meet again. Not in so many words - just a mental *'Glasnost'* between a Russian-Venusian and an English-Marstian. We proved the theory that if there's one time when the two species can lock tentacles and reach an agreement, it's when we agree to go our separate ways.

CASEBOOK NO:4:-

The following day, I made the 20min journey from Reading to Basingstoke where I met up with Nina. 2 dates in 24hrs - life had gone into overdrive. One of the reasons I had previously declined to meet the other Basingstoke lass was because I was already talking to Nina and if I was ever to venture thus far, it would be to meet the latter lady. And so it came to be that I - ageing but cute, inquisitive but polite, nervous but excited - was to meet a delightful 27yr-old in a bar outside Basingstoke railway station. 27 - back of the net! At this stage I need to point out that Nina was not her real name. At first, I was aggrieved to discover this as not only had I felt that she had lied to me, but, it also rendered my original ditty to her utterly meaningless. So, for the record (gulp), here is that ditty:

"There was a young lass name of Nina, So pretty - you'd agree if you'd seen her. Full of fun and ideas, And admired by her peers, A true miss not a true misdemeanour!"

OK, you can laugh but bearing in mind I was wearing vodka glasses late at night and needed to 'upsell' myself, I thought it wasn't bad and it certainly had the desired effect. Nina sounded fun. Her outlook on life was refreshing. She sounded open-minded, intelligent and a real people person. I wasn't to be disappointed. I chatted with this delightful young lady for 2hrs and learnt about her passion for spirituality, travel, music and her ambition to sing. She had emerged from a stifling relationship and was taking time out to blossom and enjoy herself. So, why was she telling this to a strange Marstian - 14yrs her senior at the time - who could turn out to be, well, just about anybody? It was then it struck me just how brave she was to have even agreed to meet in the first place. Blind dates are pretty daunting at the best of times but most Earth-beings who have undertaken them, did so at a time of life when the fear-factor simply didn't exist. Youth. But here was a Venusian who, like her distant relatives, was prepared to try and communicate with her opposite number without prejudice, no matter what cards her young life had already dealt her. Being a red-blooded male from the red-bloody planet, I was - quite naturally - attracted to Nina, whose pseudonym came courtesy of Nina Simone, a mutual love of Ms Simone being one of many interests we shared. But a prolonged friendship was the best I could hope for and it was as good friends we parted .... never to meet again. We communicated via e-mail and text for a while until I suddenly became aware that the communication process was only flowing one way. Was it a healthy scenario for me to try and keep in touch with a girl so much younger? Haven't 27yr-olds built up enough friends so as not to require the attentions of another, more maturer individual? Does she believe that friendship is impossible without the 'When Harry Met Sally' syndrome, of which so many previous Marstians have been guilty? Who, knows. All I do know is Nina saw me without my paper bag and, more importantly, without that t-shirt/suit combo. And the questions remain unanswered. I deleted her mobile number and e-mail address and thought, if she wants to talk, she'll contact me. She didn't.

CASEBOOK NO:5:- At the time of writing, there is no casebook No:5. But maybe - just maybe - a 5th and hopefully final casebook, may have taken place before the end of the book. So, watch this space. Sorry, I mean look at the back page.

TAKE ON BOARD - A barristers wig. Then, you can be Judge Mental when you meet new Venusians, it'll make for calming, rational conversation and it means getting called to the bar on a daily basis.

CHAPTER 6: ALL VENUSIANS ARE FROM LESBOS.

It's generally been said that lesbianism was invented so big girls could find love too. Of course, this could be deemed as being a slight on the many gay-Venusians that inhabit Planet Earth 2006AD. But it has to be said, there is a huge gulf between internet lesbians and the real thing. Apparently. Whereas the type *we see pot-holing (exploring moistened underground crevasses) on the other end of our monitors are true beauties of the traditional Venusian kind, the type of carpet-muncher most of us would be likely to encounter at the counter of Tesco, is a rotund bus driver from Scunthorpe. Particularly if you shop at Tesco and/or live in Scunthorpe. But the act of lesbianism within the Venusian race acts as a threat to future Marstian kind and as we endeavour to eradicate the breakdown between the sexes and its almost apocalyptic inevitability, Marstians need to act fast to ensure that in the not-too-distant future, we are not surplus to the cause.

Now, consider the facts: When our female ancestors lived 67odd million miles from the sun, they lived in total isolation. Totally isolated from other species but comfortable within their own environment, with their own kind. As previously stated, having had their planet hi-jacked by a spaceship full of Marstians, they discovered new feelings, new emotions, new priorities. But having travelled to Earth and had their population diluted by 50%, Venusians have now started to look back at what they had before - a world without men. On Venus, the female of the species hoped there was more to life than endless suntans and although conventional sex was impossible and unheard of until the invasion by the penile sector, they knew what they liked and feminine lust had long since found a form. But things were different on the Red Planet. With the help of their telescopic lenses, the male gender were satisfying their needs thanks to the help of their neighbours, 120million km down the road. So, the entire future of the human race were getting their moon-rocks off, courtesy of just 50% of the galactic population. Of course, there is no evidence to suggest that our male ancestors didn't enjoy the pleasures of botty-love on Planet Mars but rumour has it, this wasn't risked because of the impending long-distance space journey where all males would have to be seated for a very long time! So, Planet Earth in the 21st Century. Women have discovered that sex without men is oh-so-much better. Men have long since discovered that sex with one is better than sex with two (this includes the man himself), but the inspiration behind their own form of self-abuse is still, quintessentially, the woman. As is the case for the girlies. When they find those erogenous zones that mankind's creator put in the most ludicrous of places, Angeline Jolie is at the forefront of their mind. Proof - go for a night out, have a few beers and get talking to both sexes about sex. Ask any lady - after midnight and 8 Vodka & Red Bull's - what woman they fancy and they won't even question your question. They will think, ponder, giggle and then announce in true girly fashion "that girl from Tomb Raider (lol)". Normal procedure means that they will then denounce any further sexual attraction but having discovered that her best mate fancies Miss Jolie too, she will then state "well, if I'd had a few drinks". Now guys. Ask a bloke - after midnight & 8 pints of lager - which Rogers they'd like to roger and you probably already know the outcome: 2 broken teeth, a fractured eye-socket, severely bruised ribs and an ashtray inserted into the rectal passage. But I got it out OK.

So guys, we have to ask ourselves - are we in danger of losing our other halves (or three-quarters if they are aged 35 or over) to another distant galaxy? With George W.Bush's current space programme sending Venusians into orbit on a fairly regular basis, we have to ask ourselves - why? Up until July 26th 2005, as many as 40 women had flown into space and although female astronauts are generally spread thinly on the ground (particularly the ones who travelled in the Shuttle), it shows how far the space-race has progressed since the Russian Urine Gagari became the first man in space in 1961. As stated in Chapter 1, space travel - or more specifically, space travel to the moon - is very much an archaic form of world exploration. We are now spending more time trying to stop the inevitable destruction of our own planet courtesy of global warming, rather than search for pastures new. (Please omit the aforementioned Mr. Bush from that statement, as he continues to destroy as much of Planet

Earth as is feasibly possible from the confines of his office).

BUSH (derivative)
1. Woody plant between <u>a</u> tree and an under shrub in size; a shrub <u>thick</u> with branches; anything of bushy tuftlike shape; forest; <u>wild uncultivated</u> county; such <u>country</u> covered with bushes; the wild.
<u>Don't you just love politics?</u>

So, at a time when asbo's, illegal immigrants, global warming and Jade Goody dominate the news, why is Mr. Shrub and his Russian nemesis continuing to send peeps into space, a large percentage of whom are of the Venusian gender?

What is the Venusian version of an un-manned space probe?

Answer: A dildo!

I digress again. Russian cosmonaut Valentina Tereshkova became the first woman in space on June 18th 1963. During her 71hrs aboard Vostok 6, she circled the Earth no fewer than 48 times (fact). The Russian authorities realised that this replicated the actions of a Muscovite Venusian trying to find a parking space for her Trabant and as this contradicted their pioneering spirit, it would be another 19yrs before the female form donned a spacesuit again. So, up until 1982, women (or that should read 'woman') made up only a tiny percentage of all peeps who had participated in the 'space-race', although that terminology was to take on a whole new meaning as other nations realised that the cosmos wasn't exclusive to just Americans & Russians. But just as the percentage had diminished to that of a fraction and Ms Tereshkova faded from the memory (assisted by Russian vodka and American propaganda), a second female cosmonaut was launched into the Solar System and things started to change. As previously stated, as many as 40 women have now flown into space - that is approximately 9% of all astronauts/cosmonauts. So, what is happening? Are women looking for a way back to their distant homeland, albeit some millions of kilometres away? Let's face it, they left behind a dry, arid, wasteland that was devoid of respite from the sun, devoid of male companionship and without the most precious commodity known to man - water. They came to Planet Earth to start a new life, to live in harmony with another alien life-form, to reap the harvest of a fertile & lush planet and to pro-create because without the necessary seed, the Venusians could no longer exist as a single species. But now, hundreds of years on, Venusians find themselves on Earth: an arid wasteland, due to years of war and conflict between various factions of Marstians. Earth: a planet devoid of respite from the sun, due to a f***ing great big hole in the ozone layer caused by aerosols and arseoles (the aerosols were weapons of mass destruction wielded by the breasted ones in the 1980's, as they searched for the Holy Grail that was - 'big hair'). Earth: a planet devoid of male companionship because those constant, communicative companions from many moons ago have turned into hunter-gatherers and explorers, in a constant search for something new, bigger, better, faster & shinier. As previously stated, having stepped outside of the comfort zone of the new world they'd helped to create, man is now finding it difficult to step back in. More than ever before, the Marstian race is totally alien to that of the Venusian one.

How many people have flown in space? That was a question I asked Google because somewhere along the line, my readers deserve some good hard facts. Hopeful of a simple answer, I was offered no fewer than 6,350,000 pages of options - hardly a 'googlewhack'. It's amazing that a sentence constructed out of 7 words can return that many hits yet the words clotted, cream and anal can only generate approximately 10,600 pages of interest. Apparently. But interest in space travel and the quest to renew life on Mars & Venus is now more popular than ever and what was deemed as testosterone-fuelled acts of bravado some 30-40yrs ago, is now seen as a family day out. More and more people from all corners of the globe are venturing skywards and 37yrs after Neil Armstrong supposedly ended the space-race by 'being there, doing that and wearing the t-shirt', the race is on in earnest again. But this isn't America v Russia.....this is man v woman. But (and this is a BIG but, otherwise known as a 'J-Lo'), do the Venusians have what it takes to make that journey back home? Yes, their brains evolved at an alarming rate throughout the 20th Century and they now have a firm grasp (and they always grasp too firmly!) of the physics and diagnostics involved to get that baby off the ground. Yes, having created that huge orifice in the Earth's protective shield, they now have a clear sight of the land they once called home. And yes, they will use SatNav AND a map so don't underestimate just how far they can go. But in the cold light of day, the Venusians do not yet have what it takes to escape the tentacles of the Marstian race on our war-ravaged planet. Take a look at this:

- Nearly 10% of all space travellers have been women.
- Not including those killed whilst on the ground, space disasters have killed around 20 people, which equates to approximately 5% of all travellers. But:
- 10% of all women who have undertaken space travel, have died, which is twice the average.
- And as 4 of those 20 fatalities (see above) were women, no fewer than **20%** of all space travellers who failed to have their return ticket stamped, were women.

So, if those statistics represent 2 decades+ of Venusians as the proverbial back-seat drivers, just imagine what could happen when they finally get the chance to adjust the drivers seat, slap on a 'Westlife' CD, do their 'lippy' and take control of the cosmos? They haven't conquered the skies yet, so it's up to us Marstians to ensure that their willpower matches their driving prowess. And if we all keep our pod-shaped feet on the ground, it may not yet be the end of civilisation as we know it.

*The term 'we' is used here purely to bring in those Venusians/Marstians that haven't had to endure the horrors of lesbianism, visually or physically. Sacrifices were made during the compilation of this book.

TAKE ON BOARD - Angeline Jolie.

CHAPTER 7: ARE YOU FOR REAL?

I have discussed many different forms of the communication process earlier in this book and its become quite apparent that the more tools we are equipped with to aid the art of communication, the less we know how to utilise them. Mobile phones, MSN, e-mail - they all come with guidance and instructions but are we really making the connection? Yes, we do talk more than ever before but are we still speaking the same language?

Although the Oxford English Dictionary continues to expand at a rate of knots with new words, phrases and definitions added on an annual basis, our ability to nurture and expand our own vocabulary diminishes by the day. We are no longer either willing or able to construct a meaningful conversation. And when we try, we don't always say what we should have said. Or tell the truth. Whilst the other 5 major languages of the world (Spanish, Arabic, French, Mandarin-Chinese & Hindi) have generally managed to keep their native tongue as a simplistic form of communication - devoid of hidden meanings, double entendres and misunderstanding - the largely English speaking world have managed to develop it to a stage where the basic structure of our language has imploded. We struggle to talk. This struggle, allied with the aforementioned technology and the natural evolutionary paths our forms have taken, make a future together on this unearthly planet, nigh on impossible.

There are still strange scenario's played out on a daily basis where we manage to talk, but when your average Marstian (5ft11", £24,000pa, Man. United supporting, beer-bellied, gadget-freak) meets an average Venusian (smaller, smaller still, definitely not, yuk, oooh yes) in any of the following situations, the following interaction usually takes place:

Marstian to Venusian at bus-stop: *"They say it's gonna rain later"* Doh!

Venusian to Marstian washing car: *"You can do mine as well if you want"* (lol)

Marstian to Venusian in garage: *"Your big-end's gone"*

Venusian to Marstian in a club: *"No thanks, I'm just waiting for my mate"*

Venusian to Marstian in bedroom: *"Just turn around a minute, you've got a huge zit on your back"* (No? Obviously just me then)

But what's the point? Why can't we say what we really think? Why have we lost the ability to make the most of every speaking moment? Years ago, when there was nothing to talk about, people spoke. Now, with senses working overtime due to an overload of data, we say nothing of interest.

This is what we should be saying:

Marstian to Venusian at bus-stop: *"Apparently, I think about sex every 8 seconds so by the time you've mounted the*

No.69, I would have plugged every single orifice in your body!"

Venusian to Marstian washing car: *"If it's true what they say about blokes with big cars, you certainly won't need a sponge that big when you're in the shower!"*

Marstian to Venusian in garage: *"When I return in a future life, I want to come back as a lumberjack. Chopping down trees all day sounds such fun. Do you believe in the afterlife? What do you think about the rain-forests? Don't run away......"*

Venusian to Marstian in a club: *"Hello pimple-face. You look like a skateboarder if ever I've seen one. Tell me about your day?"*

Marstian to Venusian in bedroom: *"Your big-end's gone!"*

The following are genuine testimonies from ladies who shared their experiences, with a total stranger, regarding their on-line experiences. Word-for-word, these are their tales of how on-line Marstians were truly more horrific than those they had met in the green, scaley flesh.

"Yes, my book will be out first I think been on here too long and just seem to find the 'married but they don't know it' ones or have lost wife to cult or crack or in the cupboard with Harry Potter under stairs! Where are the non-freaky non-geeky straight guys who don't dress up in their dead mothers clothes? Or have more issues and baggage than gatwick?"
MANDY (39) from Sutton. (JULY 2005)
For those horticulturists among you, Sutton is a place where you can pick up lots of bags full of seed.

*"Well Phil,, the whole internet dating thing has been...
interesting...lol. I have found its amazing how many
'forget' they're married when filling out their profiles and
it would appear that fixations on underwear or lack of it
is also a common theme...lol. Honest, you don't wanna get
me started!!! But in true Dunkirk spirit, I forge onwards,
still searching for that illusive 'something' or 'someone'...lol"*
(JULY 2005)
*SANDRA (35) from Portsmouth which, apparently, is full
of discharged seamen.*

*"Can't believe some of the messages i've received and if
anything, my faith in men has diminished more than
ever! Received over 150 messages when I first joined this
site but by the time i'd trawled thru all of the usual
'fancy a f**k-buddy' requests and inane and somewhat
scary comments about my kids and single status, I felt
like quitting the site. Your messages have been amongst
the few decent ones i've received. This is certainly an
easy way to meet new people but so far, they seem like
people i'd rather not meet. Hope you are 'avin better
luck than me (lol)!"*
JADE (36) from Birmingham. Unfunny.

So, what is it about Mars-tians and their appalling
memory? It has been scientifically proven that the two
alien life-forms digest information in different ways.
The male is more likely to absorb information related
to him by a member of his own sex because he has
a natural defence mechanism called 'Anti-Trivialism',
which deflects anything that doesn't relate to **L**)
Football, **A**) Sex, **B**) Cars, **I**) Money or **A**) Sex into

the green room which lies at the back of his huge, but largely unused, brain. Apparently, men think about sex approximately every 8 seconds. If so, a life-span of 64yrs will encompass a whole <u>8 years</u> of just thinking about the art of copulation. Bearing in mind that any 64yr-old bloke should have lived through at least 24yrs where sex was either illegal or physically impossible (please note the term 'should' - ask your Grandad if he had sex before leaving school or whether he's got jiggy with it since yer Gran dried up from a grape to a sultana), this accounts for a total of 32yrs, or half of his life. And we haven't even begun to take into account the amount of time when the seed was actually freed, regardless or not whether there was somebody on the receiving end! So, sex is an integral, permanent presence in the Marstian brain.

(Any mathematicians/doctors reading will have noticed that the 8yrs taken into account includes those very years where I've stated that sex was illegal (0-15) and where sex is a tad more difficult (55-64). But for people in these age ranges, although the thought of it is just as prevalent, the dreams of young boys and what they are gonna do to the opposite sex and the memories of old boys and what they did in their younger days, are somewhat clouded and misguided. So, the maths does add up. Sort of. As for you doctors, yes - I know, it's now legal to have sex at the age of 12 and Viagra helps sustain a longer sex life but in the 2000+years we have existed on Planet Earth, this data is far more accurate. Anyway, it's a well-known fact that doctors and mathematicians - along with naturists, tracton-engine drivers and Cliff Richard's fan-club - don't get any sex either).

> *"men hav nipples so they can practice tweaking them and yanking them to get in practice for wen they get lucky and get a chick. Met 3 guys through these sites. one never stopped blinking. the 2nd had bigger tits than me and came harmed wif 30 condoms. the 3rd I dated 4 2months, he thought he was don corleone, ducking and diving, went wrong wen he asked me to lend him a grand. wouldn't tell me why he needed it. i told him to take the next plane to sicily"*
>
> *LISA (34) from Hindhead (is that where the term 'talking out of the arse' originates from?*

Apart from answering the question as to why men have nipples, Lisa failed to answer the question as to how many condoms geezer No:2 actually went home with.

> *"im a right down 2 earth girl meet few sick people in the head on ths wht mks them tick pervs, lol i could tell us a few stories"*
>
> *ANAHRISHA (34) from - well, must be Barking*
>
> *Here is a rough translation of the above sentence:*
> *"I'm a right down-to-earth girl. I've met a few people who were sick-in-the head, on this site. What makes them tick? Pervs! (chuckle) I could tell you a few stories"*

As you will see from my research, the only feedback I received came from ladies in a similar age-group to that of myself. I would have quite liked to have surveyed women of a younger age but e-mailing total strangers half my age and asking them if they've ever had correspondence with any pervy or crank geezers is a bit like asking a suicide bomber "What makes you tick?" - asking for trouble. So, although this research isn't as expansive as I'd wish, I believe it gives a fair reflection of the way the Marstian species interprets its opposite number.

TAKE ON BOARD: A lie-detector. With electrodes attached to the genitalia. The truth must be sought but let's enjoy the hunt.

CHAPTER 8: BODY TALK:
TALKING OUT OF YOUR.....

When the first Venusians & Marstians touched down on Earth many moons ago, interpreting or understanding the body of their opposite species soon became paramount. Not just the physical form but the signals it was actually transmitting. With every grunt, every sound, came expression and movement and our ancestors took the time to decipher this amalgam of signals. Then, having reached a plateau on which both sexes could communicate, they progressed from touching down to touching up, via that mutual touching of tentacles.

Forward 2000yrs. Body Language is as prevalent as ever and whilst our everyday sub-conscious use of body language as a form of communication is an integral part of meeting/greeting/mating/dating/talking/discussing/complaining/gusset etc, our own ability to understand the signals has diminished over time.

There is a generally held belief that the spoken word now makes up just 7% of the communication process. The other 93% is made up of the tone in which the words are spoken and the actual Body Language Transmission (stance, hand-signals etc) which - for the purpose of practicality - is generally known as a BLT. The brain, as discussed in various other parts of this fantastic journal, is key to all things relative to the communication process. The human brain is the central organ of our nervous system and much of it is largely unused. This is a sweeping, factual statement and is not reserved for 'Big Brother' contestants, footballers wives and Albanians. The brain is divided into chambers and each section absorbs and/or stores different everyday stimuli such as memory, movement and emotion. In this fast-moving world of ours, our brain has to respond to our nervous system and the various sights, sounds, tastes and smells that swamp our body every micro-second of the day. As previously stated, the male brain is larger than that of the fairer sex but as they so readily tell those of us of the penile sector who are more than equipped for the job in hand (metaphorically speaking of course), "its not about size, it's what you do with it". And they then tell the less-endowed members of the Marstian race (known as bite-size), "it is about size!". Oh, Mr Digression has shoved his finger up my anus again. The Brain. Oh yes, so it's fair to say that the male brain is a largely unused piece of marshmallow and as stated in Chapter 7, it only absorbs a percentage of its working capacity. So, if the male brain is more receptive to the voice of a fellow Marstian than that of a Venusian, it is already under performing by 50%. Venusians, being a tad more communicative than our good selves - hence the book - listen, understand and respond to data from all species in a far more productive way. Exam results bear this out, with female students far outperforming their male counterparts on a yearly basis.

And then there's the aforementioned body language. It's patently obvious that Marstians do not have the necessary antennae to read the signals which constitute 93% of the communication process. Hence the fact that when <u>she</u> says "don't forget to pick the kids up", <u>he</u> only hears the words that are spoken. This is how the message is received in the brain of a Brian:

"Don't forget to pick the kids up" data-read-data…... process information……don't understand gesticulation, eliminate from information process…..data-read…... ignore raised voice and emphasis on words at end of sentence, because she is always moaning…..data-read-data….kids..pick-up..kids….data emanating from Venusian source….reduce GPRS signal by 50%…. data-read….process response, process response, process response……………………………….....

"Pardon?"

So, whereas many ladies have been known to choke when it comes to oral examinations, the guys are quite simply hopeless and fail every time. 93% of the original message has already been put through the head-shredder and the remaining data is then cut by half, leaving a 3.5% margin - or a less than 1 in 25 chance - of Jack & Jill actually getting collected from their after school activities!

Imagine the following scene which is actively played out on a weekly basis in most bars throughout London which, as you'll understand from the body map described in the second chapter, is a throbbing metropolis where anything can - and probably will - happen:

Geezer talks to a Venusian of the more 'shapely' form. But does he notice the furtive eye movement that, despite her obvious shyness, suggests she is interested in the attention that she's receiving? Does he notice the way she playfully runs her fingers through her hair, language which subconsciously sends out teasing messages pertaining to her sexuality and does he notice the way she angles her head in his general direction, which screams "I'm interested in you?" And that a shag may not be entirely out of the question? Does he heck. His reading of the situation is summed up on his return to his Burberry-clad crowd of mates, when he loudly declares "she likes chips, no wot I mean like (lol)". If we are that crap at interpreting the messages that positively radiate from our opposite numbers, what hope is there for us when we attempt to romance via e-mail or MSN, when the written word suddenly takes on an even greater intensity? When a Venusian 'on-liner' picks up a romantic message from the other end of her computer, she'll imagine that her potential suitor only has eyes for her. He would have trawled through her profile to ensure compatibility and he'll be sat, glass of vintage cognac in hand, with hands, feet, head and antennae all pointing at the screen, along with Cupid's bow of course. But the following is the cold, hard truth:

"Ohhh, thank god for that, was beginning to think it was me attracting the wrong sort only...lol lol...webcam...well lets just say I had chatted to the guy for weeks, never a mention of anything sordid, got on really well, liked him too, very attractive with his e-mails etc, one day says he has webcam, (we had progressed to MSN by then) so I (like a fool) accept and he is butt naked...with a very large stiff erm ya know and doing his favourite pastime!!!...

*closed window down, told him was not on here for that
(mind it was impressive lol lol) and after that sort of
avoided him...he soon got the message...though I do admit
to laughing about it with girlfriends after...but that was
an eye-opener and i have a couple more friends I talk to
now on MSN from these sites made it clear don't ever do
anything like that or I'm off. Had a few photo's of adult
nature sent too, and again...blocked the guys...on here to
find good friends and one person special not someone who
just wants to messa bout...makes me mad that people who
are supposed to be mature act like bloody kids. anyway,
forget the Pringles...will take the vodka...these sites have
driven me to drink lol lol x"*
JULIA (JULY 2005)

Sex. My talking about it is akin to Jordan holding court with virgins and discussing chastity. Basically, I am out of touch. But its those of us not currently splitting the whiskers of the female gender who are probably best equipped to talk about it. And believe you me, talking about it is something we all do. Venusians and Marstians alike will quite happily discuss the merits of a shagged one, with a fellow being. E.g: male tells male about the 'bird' he bonked and just how dirty she was, forgetting to mention the fact that she was in fact very grubby and needed bookends to keep her legs from collapsing to a 180degree angle. Meanwhile, female tells female about the size of the Marstian who skewered her the night before and how, for the first time in ages (minutes/hours/ days/weeks - delete as necessary ladies), batteries were not required. But then suddenly things change. What happens if bookend girl ain't so bad after all and she turns out to be pretty handy with the microwave and a tin of Mr.Sheen? And what happens if the guy with the salami turns out to be a humorous, honest, loving and faithful man of substance? Ha ha ha. Oh deary me. Anyway, all of a sudden, the conversations change course. We no longer want our pals and workmates to know the sexual merits of our partners. No, we want you to meet them now. He wants to take bookend girl to the pub quiz and she wants to bring salami man to her sisters BBQ. So what has happened? Well, we have suddenly allowed the chamber of our brain marked 'Love', to override the section marked 'Sex'. In the grey-matter belonging to the Venusian-race, this is a fairly simple process because the two are inexplicably linked and the element of the brain marked 'Love' has authority over all others. But in the brain of a Brian, it is a totally different and far more complex scenario. 'Sex' features prominently in the front lobe of the brain and the few other areas that are fully-operational tend to be full of 'Football', 'Beer' and 'Miscellanous'. 'Love' is filed under miscellaneous. When a woman falls in love, the force of it affects her whole nervous system and she suddenly gains the ability to giggle, fall over and gaze for hours. The 'Beer' section in the mans brain has a similar effect. A chamber entitled 'Shoes' follows close behind 'Love' in the female brain and then there's the 'Sex' section which tends to lie dormant, until 'Love' has been fully activated. Still with me? But in the male brain, the 'Love' section has to fight its way through a mass of obstacles and takes far longer to become fully functional. It receives its stimuli via the chamber marked 'Sex' and eventually, the cells unite to force other active areas - 'Football' & 'Beer' - to the rear section of the brain. This process of brain prioritisation is known as 'BILLYNOMATITIS'. Eventually!!!!!!!

Venusians love to be loved. This strong and deepest of emotions harks back to their most primitive of instincts. When the Martians (confectionery joke stops now) first landed on Venus and scooped up these beautiful beings in a mass of tentaclae and testiculae, the Venusians showed a vulnerability that was to set a benchmark for woman-kind. Think Richard Gere at the end of 'An Officer and a Gentleman', think knight in shining armour and his damsel in distress. Love brings a feeling of security and no matter how the Venusian race has acclimatised and evolved over the past 2000yrs, that feeling of need forever remains in their mutant genes. They will always be the weaker sex physically - give or take the odd East-European athlete - and unless we start experimenting in threesomes with beings from yet another planet, the bodily form in which both races currently exist, is unlikely to change.

The Martian race needs love too. But hunter-gatherers though they may be, love has never quite topped their shopping list. Our female ancestors felt almost powerless within the presence of the invaders from afar, particularly once they had been taken away from the environment they had called home for so long. It was the Martians who had built the spaceship which was to change their lives forever and they felt indebted to these bigger, stronger, smellier beings from along the galaxy. That feeling of superiority that the early Venusian settlers (the word 'settlers' is derived from the fact that they never had headaches and always gave 'express relief') bestowed on their counterparts remains till this day and although Venusians can now read, write and run countries, they are still driven by that basic need to be clubbed on the head with a cudgel and dragged off into the nearest cave.

So, signals deciphered, juices swapped, acclimatisation complete. But man had to conquer this brave new world called Earth. There were things to build, things to plant, things to seek and things to kill. But they had to return every 8 seconds to park the pork. But as they ventured further into this strangest of strange lands, the bungee on their ballbag became untethered and return visits became more intermittent. And when they did return, the most primal of male instincts took over from those warm, romantic liasons previously shared with the Venusian beings. The process of 'Selective Amnesia' had started and both sets of beings were already forgetting all they'd learnt about their opposite number and discovering a new life. Alone.

*Where does the term 'fairer' sex come from? They are only fair if there's no fare.....and thats not usually the case.

TAKE ON BOARD: A toolbox. We keep ours in the garage, they keep theirs in the bedside drawer. We needs loads of spanners because a lot of nuts will need tightening but hide their screwdrivers, because they are getting a bit tasty with this DIY lark.

CHAPTER 9: EXODUS/NO WOMAN, NO CRY

The Bible, 'The Origin Of Species' or 'Men Are from Mars, Women Are From Venus'. Which would you read? Two of them are renowned works of fiction based on a Martian perception of where our true origins lie but the third book is a groundbreaking piece of script that shoots straight at the heart of doubt and cynicism. Religion is not to be mocked (and I will do my upmost not to do this) and to avoid upsetting any readers or incurring a fatwah on my head, I will tread carefully whilst comparing the various faiths & beliefs and how they impact on the man v woman fight for survival. Christianity has been the axis on which much of our learnings and beliefs have been based upon and all over the world, this simplistic ideal of how and why we are here is still preached to this day.

Christianity remains the worlds biggest religion and in 2002, there were reported to be approximately 2billion Christians, in nearly all parts of the world. But the 'good book' is no longer welcome in every corner of the globe and although Christianity is still rife in the largely democratic Western world, a lack of indoctrination has made this 2000yr-old belief a somewhat minority sport. For much of the Western world - the very territory where Martians and Venusians are losing the battle to co-exist - our religious beliefs continue to impact little on our daily lives. So, is the alliance of Christianity and democracy as bedfellows, to blame for our current state of affairs? Faith is a fundamental part of any religion and although many Westerners only seek solace in their belief as and when it suits them, its very prescence reaffirms that each and every one of us has some understanding of why we may be here.

You gotta have faith, ooooooooo you gotta have faith, faith, faith.

But modern times and thinking have seen the publication of 'The Origin Of Species' & 'Men Are From Mars etc', books that have rocked the very foundation of the Christian world, as well as that of other religions.

First published on November 24, 1859, ***The Origin of Species*** (full title ***On the Origin of Species by Means of Natural Selection, or the Preservation of Favoured Races in the Struggle for Life***) by English naturalist Charles Darwin is one of the pivotal works in scientific history, In it, Darwin argues his theory that groups of organisms, rather than individual organisms, gradually evolve through the process of natural selection. In other words, we have descended from apes. This challenged the Victorian held beliefs regarding our whole existence and it attracted widespread interest on publication, causing a furor into the bargain. Nearly a century-and-a-half later and nobody would dare write such a book because to do so would challenge the intolerance of some of the more extreme religions and their breakaway factions, the likes of which had never bothered our Vicky. But if we might not have been singing from the same songsheet before, we most certainly aren't now. Whether you were a Carpenters (Bible) fan or a Monkees ('Origin Of Species') fan, nothing could have prepared folks for what was to become the Sex Pistols of the literary world - 'Men Are From Mars, Women Are From Venus'.

Jokes abound regarding the immaculate conception and the birth of our saviour in a stable. But in the year 2006AD with babies being created for gay couples and NHS hospitals closing on an almost daily basis, it doesn't look quite so daft now does it!? But what about Adam's rib? Do you honestly believe that a bloke would give a stranger a good bone, in the vein (deliberate spelling error) hope of improving his sex life with another? OK, maybe the Bible isn't as fictional as originally stated............

........which leads us onto this gag. Great joke, you may have heard it before but a) it's appropriate (for those of you who believe 'Adams Rib' to be a bistro) b) we need to lighten the tone and c) it's my book. Sorry, there was no need for that.

Adam was walking around the Garden of Eden feeling very lonely, so God asked Adam, "What is wrong with you?". Adam said he didn't have anyone to talk to. God said he was going to give him a companion and it would be a woman. He said, "This woman will cook for you and wash your clothes, she will always agree with every decision you make. She will bear you children and never ask you to get up in the middle of the night to take care of them. She will not nag you and will always be the first to admit she was wrong when you've had a disagreement. She will never have a headache and will

freely give you love, sex and compassion whenever needed."
Adam asked God, "What will a woman like this cost?" God
said, "An arm and a leg." Adam said, "What can I get for
just a rib?" The rest is history.

So, if you are not a Christian, what are you? Well,
apart from the 2billion Christians mentioned above, the
2002 census also reported there to be more than 1billion
Muslims, nearly 830million Hindu's and more than
360million Buddhists. The message of Islam is gradually
being spread across the world but most of its followers
continue to exist exclusively in parts of Africa & Asia.
Hinduism is found mainly in India but has been exported
too, courtesy of the peoples indiginous to that country.
And 98% of all Buddhists can be found in Asia. As stated
in Chapter 4, it is in some of the worlds poorest nations
that man and woman continue to live side-by-side in
relative harmony and a huge proportion of those people
are stronger in faith than they are of material wealth.
As previously stated, less is more and more is less. That
more or less makes sense I think. But from the time
that first spaceship spluttered to Earth with its cargo of
thirsty Venusians, horny Marstians and a Rottweiller
called Fang, the evolution process has taken different
courses. In the powerful nations of the Western world,
communication has largely broken down because while
the men were venturing further afield to find bigger and
better, the women escaped their leash and did likewise.
Without the shackles of an indoctrinated culture or creed
that would punish them, they sought their own destiny
and are partly to blame for the situation we now find
ourselves in 2006AD. So, can we learn from some of the
poorer nations, where family values and faith guide each

and every waking moment? Well maybe. But look at it this way ladies, in many of these countries, Venusians are - and always have been - second-class citizens. Many Venusians have to walk several paces behind their 'master'. Many Venusians have to cover their legs and their faces. Many Venusians are deprived of education and the ability to achieve. Many Venusians have to share their husband with many other wives. And many Venusians are forced into arranged or illegal marriages whilst others are stoned to death if they dare stray outside of it. So ladies, we do need your help on this one.

So, where else is there to go? Well, we can't go back. Mars was left in a pretty sorry state and Venus is now hotter than ever. Ideally, this prolonged battle of the sexes (and you thought the 100-year war was long) will reach a pointless conclusion and after years of hostility, we'll agree a truce and all sit down and have a nice cup of tea together. Anybody who watches English Test cricket will be familiar with this scenario. But we may have to flee our planet and bugger off anyway, in which case here are some of the possible alternatives. Think of this as a cross between Noah's Ark and The Muppets In Space:

JUPITER: Sometimes referred to as the 'king of the planets', Jupiter is the first of the 4 gas planets and is the 5th planet from the sun. It is the daddy of the cosmos and has 61 moons. Bearing in mind that this would be the most accessible land outside the 4 terrestrial planets (Mercury/Venus/Earth/Mars) and it has the largest capacity of anything in the solar system, this

would be the most obvious place for us to send our ships if a mass exodus is required. It has a rocky core 10/20 times as massive as Earth, so landing maybe tricky. Above this is metallic and then liquid hydrogen, topped by about 1,000km of atmosphere, 86% of which is hydrogen and 14% helium (yawnnnnnnnn). Jupiter's narrow ring system, discovered as recently as 1979, consists of 3 rings of dust particles.

(In Roman mythology, Jupiter - the offspring of Saturn - was king of the gods. A sky god, he was associated with thunderbolts, lightning and victory in war, making him a pretty scarey muther. And he married his own sister!).

My god, isn't astronomy boring?

Taking all of the above information into account and thinking back to what we (sorry, YOU) have learnt in the preceeding 8 chapters, I recommend that the following peeps should disembark at Jupiter: Royalty, in-breds, world leaders/politicians, claustrophobes, Kim or Aggie, sun-worshippers, the gay community, Joe Pasquale, naturists and all people who weigh more than 20stone.

SATURN: Saturn is the second-largest planet and the 6th from the sun. Like Jupiter, it is composed chiefly of hydrogen surrounding a rocky core. Its mass is so spread out that it has the lowest density of all the planets. Saturn is best known for its extensive ring system and it's this almost mystical image of Saturn, that helps bring astronomy to a younger audience. And the Moon with his smiley face. These thousands of ringlets are made up of ice-covered rock and dust particles. The particles range from a few thousandths of a centimetre to a few miles across and the whole system is up to 2km thick.

(In Roman mythology, Saturn was an ancient god - possibly of agriculture. Suppose somebody had to do it. He was dethroned by his sons Jupiter, Neptune & Pluto, making him a bit of a wuss).

Isn't it amazing that a Martian can measure a microscopic ringlet of rock/dust from millions of miles away, yet asked about the size of his won genitalia, would err by approximately 25%!

Taking all of the above info into account, here is the next list of passengers to disembark, if they haven't snuffed it already: Farmers, BT engineers, children, ice-skaters, Kim or Aggie, lily-livers, Italians, any politicians that previously abstained, Stephen Hawking and all people who weigh between 14-20stone.

URANUS: This planet was discovered in 1781 by a Martian called Herschel. It is twice as far from the sun as Saturn and has a ring system and 27 moons. The first close up views of Uranus came in 1986 from the probe 'Voyager 2'. Its atmosphere is predominantly hydrogen but methane in the upper clouds gives Uranus its "distinctive" bluey-green colour. Clouds of frozen methane are the only visible features and oh yes, it's cold: -210degrees centigrade/-378 degress fahrenheit at the cloud tops.

(In Greek mythology, Uranus was the sky god responsible for the sun and rain. He was the son and husband of Gaia -are you keeping up? -by whom he fathered the Titans).

Please notice I quote the word distinctive. What is "distinctive" about something that nobody - or 99.9999999999% of anybody who's ever lived - has ever seen or wishes to see?

The spaceships are getting lighter now but the following will need to be ejected at this stop. Please mind the gap: Meteorologists (including Michael Fish, even if he has retired), the Green Party, Jennifer Lopez, Greeks, boxers, environmentalists and anybody weighing between 9-14stone.

NEPTUNE: Like Uranus, Neptune - the 8th planet - is a cold and distant world. Discovered for the first time in 1846 and finally reached by 'Voyager 2' in 1989, it's a similar size to its near neighbour and is more of a bluey colour. This is because methane in the upper atmosphere absorbs red light and reflects blue. Of course, many of you already knew that. Not. By now, all spacecraft will be struggling to maintain power in the torrid and freezing conditions. Neptune is the windiest place in the entire Solar System. Winds whizz round the planet in a westerly direction, the opposite direction to which the planet spins.

(Named after the Roman god of the sea, Neptune is the equivalent of the Greek god Poseidon. Not as good as 'The Poseidon Adventure'. Neptune was the son of Saturn and has Jupiter as a big bruv and Pluto as a little bruv).

Ok, I'm now getting bored with this......zzzzzz. Sorry, peeps to alight at Neptune should include: Sailors, the Conservative Party, female Scorpions (as in the starsign - doh), Dr Who, the inhabitants of Chicago, the film industry, Jade Goody & anybody weighing under 8stone.

Also, line-dancers, bearded ones, Elvis impersonators, racists and any 'Big Brother' contestants should have been jettisoned mid-space before now.

PLUTO: The planet Pluto was discovered by Clyde Tomburgh at the Lovell Observatory, Arizona, USA in 1930. Odd place to suddenly find it. Sad thing about this was the fact that Mr Tomburgh spent most of the rest of his life, trying to find other planets. And having made such a major discovery, was the planet named after him? Hell it was. They named it after an animated dog instead. We know little of this distant planet and since commencing this book, Pluto has actually been downgraded and is no longer officially a planet. So, if anybody does manage to make contact with Mr Tomburgh via a ouija board, best keep that quiet. Anyway, whatever you wanna call it, Pluto should be the destination for many of the dregs of society although not all of the peeps listed below necessarily fall in to that category.
(So, all things considered, the sister of Neptune, Jupiter & Pluto - Juno - became queen of the gods AND their sister-in-law. Okey-dokes).

Well, there won't be many peeps left on board now. In theory, everybody should have alighted at one of the 4 big gas planets because of the weight specifications listed above but there are some people who need to remain on board until we reach Pluto, in a couple of billion light years time. Also, there are some Americans who - pound for pound - still won't fit into any of the aforementioned weight categories. These peeps are Pluto-bound: Americans (although most would have lightened the load at Jupiter), all convicted criminals, Eskimos, agrophobics, the Disney Corporation, people with sleeping sickness, pilots, Michael Winner, North-Koreans, gingers and anybody who's ever worn a shell-suit.

TAKE ON BOARD: A copy of National Geographic magazine. To understand how and why some cultures still wanna get jiggy with it. And then talk afterwards!

CHAPTER 10: SO WHAT HAVE WE LEARNT?

"OK, everyone stand in a straight line, if you're any of these, take a step back, turn around and kindly f*** off! a player, liar, alcoholic, married, conman, drug dealer, stalker, muppet, lying b*stard, passport seeker, cam king. If all you're after is a bit of cyber action, get a life! Failing that, dial an 0900 number!! Dont want a role in your next porn movie, and not looking to audition anyone for the next comeback of porkies, so cam kings - leave it out! To the guy who said I must be looking for a meal ticket just cos I have children, am quite capable of providing for them on my own thanks, and not about todump them at the nearest childrens home just so I can have a date with you, so I hope your nuts turn square and fester at the corners and your ear holes turn to a**holes and sh*t on your shoulders! Oh and before I forget, those russians and africans that are looking for a wife or passport ...SOD OFF AND STOP MESSAGING ME!!! This is a dating site, not a get into the country free site! And for those africans that have sent me messages saying how racist I am, please re-read what

I've actually said, and please quit with the 'you're picking
on me cos I'm black' routine! It really isn't attractive.
Would love to hear from the genuine among you, if you
exist, but if I?m old enough to be your mother, you're old
enough to collect your pension, or if we're 200 miles apart,
it just isn't gonna work is it, so lets not waste
each others time! 30 - 45ish only please. If you're still
reading, hopefully you're within the genuine few on here,
so drop in and say hi, I don't bite! Well, unless you want
me to!! ;) But please, get a pic, cos until you do I'm not
replying! I've been on here a year now and heard every line
in the book, so be warned....the next asshole I meet will get
tied spread eagled in a field with honey
and birdseed and chunks of bread all over their
'manhood'..I hear seagulls are hungry this time of year!"
NICKY from Swindon (July 2006)

SELECTIVE AMNESIA: Dr.Gray stated that having
touched down on Earth, both sets of intergalactic travellers
forgot - virtually overnight - that they were supposed to
be different. All of a sudden, we could speak eachothers
language but couldn't understand it. By using the term
'selective', Dr.Gay (well, we're still not sure) infers that this
cataclysmic event was a deliberate move by both parties to
forget that we are supposed to be different. Nowadays, we
all know that Martians and Venusians have vastly different
DNA with different needs, priorities, emotions and shoes
but we all forget the 'supposed to be' part, in which case
the communication process between the 2 sexes can't
take place without the relevant 'why, who, how, what,
where?' syndrome. She will continue to ask him a) "Why
are you so late home from work?" and b) "Why do you

smell of perfume when I haven't been near you today?".
He continues to ask her c) "Why do you need another pair
of shoes?" and d) "Does your mother have to come and
stay?". These questions only have relevance if a) he works
from home, b) he smells of vaginal wipes, c) she already
has 73 pairs or d) she's dead. As for question B, the answer
is actually in the question itself. Martians and Venusians
are equally to blame for the amnesiac process. Whilst the
larger Martian brain should have a greater capacity for
memory and recollection, it has to be remembered that
drugs and alcohol have largely diminished this part of
their grey-matter and its capacity is no greater than that of
the Venusian one. Also, memory was never deemed to be
an important factor by either species when the processes
of invasion, acclimatision and evolution took place and it
soon developed a position way down the pecking order
behind the subjects listed in Chapter 8. This is largely
because 2000yrs ago, there was little worth remembering.
So, please remember (if possible) the following:
**WE ARE SUPPOSED TO BE DIFFERENT SO STOP
ASKING QUESTIONS.**

DIFFERENTIATING BETWEEN LOVE & SEX:
There is an old wives tale that says love and sex are a
common bond and that one should not be considered
without the other. This is very true because the average
female will not normally consider sex without love (not
normal) and the average male will not consider love
without sex. But if the female 'average' refers to her weight
and the male 'average' refers to the size of his manhood,
both parties will have to take what they can when they
can. As for old wives, they really can't afford to be fussy

either. As previously stated, love and sex exist as two entirely different entities within the Martian brain but there is a tenuous, sinewy link between the two within the Venusian cranium. Although research and my own sad singledom has led me to spend most of my leisure time perusing what - are generally regarded as - 'dating' websites, I have occasionally pressed the wrong button and gone on to one of the more adult-orientated sites. And the first thing that struck me (OK, the second thing) was the ratio of males to females who were scouring the world wide web for "no strings attached" sex, although there were probably a few pervs who liked their women to still have strings attached, if you know what I mean! Sorry, I will discuss that no more. Period. The reason I became aware of this was because whenever I went to view who was swapping lurid stories and pictures on-line, 4 out of 5 peeps would be from the red planet. So, Venusians <u>can</u> differentiate between love and sex but not to the same extent as their hairier peers. So, if any of you guys/geezers/ blokes etc are still dreaming of fulfilling that ultimate male fantasy of a threesome in the bedroom, chances are that you will succeed (so will she!) but only one-third of those present will be Venusian.

The amazing thing about man is that having spent the best part of 9 months trying to get out of Pandora's Box, he'll spend much of the rest of his life trying to get back in again. We love sex. If I remember rightly. As hunter-gatherers, there is no greater prize than the hunted-down honeypot and as the acclaimed German psychologist Gunter Hatherer so famously said: "if it vasn't for zee distraction of zee naked voman, man vud now be far more advanced that he actually iz". So, how do we get the Venusian race to differentiate between love and sex? Or how do we get the Martians to start associating love with sex, rather than just loving sex? Well, society and the world we live in has a lot to answer for, regarding the answer to these conundrums. Men can love and women can enjoy sex and when the two come together (which rarely happens), the chemical reaction - pheramonal, hormonal, emotional - is a wondrous experience. But we need to work harder to bring the two together. "Love and marriage, go together like a horse and carriage" somebody once said. They were probably incarcerated for their troubles but this statement is oh-so-true because in 21st Century Britain, love and marriage is as common as seeing horses pulling carriages. Fewer people are bothering to tie the knot yet it has never been easier to get betrothed and you can now get wed on mountains, in swimming pools and even whilst having a molar extracted if you so wish. 42% of all sprogs are now born out of wedlock, compared with just 12% a quarter of a century ago. Women are more career-minded, men are lazier than ever and tradition has been thrown out of the window. But if we follow our forefathers (and on Merseyside, some kids DO have 4 fathers) and pursue a course of (no sex before) marriage, both parties would be safe in the knowledge that eventually, they would be shagging somebody they truely loved. Sex with a loved one would be deemed illegal before marriage although unfortunately, that would also rule out masturbation for many of us. In the meantime, both parties should proceed to shag whoever they like and if the words "I love you" are ever uttered, just put it down to alcohol consumption. Even if you/they are teetotal. Sex is easy to acquire (yeah right!) but love isn't and the two should not be bedmates.

BEFORE MARRIAGE, ONLY HAVE SEX WITH PEOPLE YOU HATE.

GETTING A TRANSLATOR: Just over a decade ago (not sure of the equivalent in Venusian/Martian years), Dr. John Gray explained that when our ancestors first started to communicate, a translator was sometimes required to enable both parties to understand eachother. Nowadays, the only translators or 'middle-men' that help man and woman communicate are the solicitors and by then, it's too late. Another Venusian has proudly proclaimed "all men are bastards", discovered the benefits of lesbianism and achieved an NVQ in 'Building The Perfect Spaceship'. So, having somebody around to assist in the communication process could be an asset. Women love gay men, which is rather ironic in itself. Gay men provide masculinity without the normal male traits of football, beer and most significantly of all, an inability to talk the same language. Also, they don't provide a threat. Whereas the 'Harry Met Sally' syndrome takes hold whenever your average male (see Chapter 7) meets his nemesis, the only reason a shirt-lifter would want to get inside a womans knickers is if she lends them to him. *Your average gay man shares many of the cliched interests associated with the breasted ones - shopping, romance, fitness, throwaway TV and most of importantly of all, the ability to turn a blind eye whilst their partner has sex behind their back (think about it)! It is a meeting of minds because despite coming from different planets, the gay Martian has a similar make-up (sorry, couldn't resist it) to that of the hetrosexual Venusian. When a gay Martian sheathes his weapon, it isn't as a prelude to sex but as a sign that here is a space-traveller who can live in harmony with another species. But unlike those from the hot and inferior land, many Martians do actually feel threatened by their gay comrades. This is totally due to ignorance. For some unearthly reason, some guys seem to believe that the gay community have taken on a 'vow of disruption' where - having been born of normal hetrosexual blood - they have decided to have a transfusion, so sticking up 2 fingers at society because of their need to be different. And this means they should be abused, insulted and punished. Doh. It just goes to show that if man can't understand those of a different mindset but of the same gender, how can he possibly begin to understand a being that is dissimilar in every way. A woman. But this is where a go-between could come in handy. Gay and hetrosexual men happily work and live side-by-side in the Western World and are generally adored by our other four-fifths (no longer 'halves'). This isn't the case in many of the poorer nations of the world but it is in those very countries that man and woman continue to co-exist, albeit 5 paces apart. So, gay men should be utilised accordingly. They have a specific purpose. *"Everyone knew that people from Mars and people from Venus spoke different languages, so when there was a conflict, they didn't start judging or fighting but instead pulled out their phrase dictionaries to understand each other more fully. If that didn't work, they went to their homo for help".* Gay men have the brain capacity and the communication skills to bring our 2 species together. They are intelligent and its estimated that 99% of all TV presenters and 104.6% of all politicians are that way inclined. I'm hetrosexual and those percentages prove the point. He craves beef, she likes pork, so why not compromise and settle for a bit of mince?

*There is no 'average' gay man and I apologise for any unfair generalisms stated above. Anyway, its well known that unlike many of the peeps mentioned earlier in this book, gay men do indeed get plenty of sex. Unless they are Elvis impersonators, traffic wardens etc.

GAY MEN - EVERY HOME SHOULD HAVE ONE!

Stop Press...Stop Press.....Latest on-line news......

- Women have suddenly discovered an irrational passion for the movie 'White Chicks'.
- Beware the con they call 'Fast Flirt' or 'Carpet Bomb'. On-line dating sites encourage their subscribers to send out a generic message which will be forwarded to up to 100 peeps that fit your specifications. So, if your ideal woman is a 5ft 5" redhead who earns loadsa money and lives within 50 miles, you can send the same message (e'g "Yo bitch, wanna get jiggy wit me?") to up to 100 women who fit that category. But on closer inspection, you'll notice that barely any of these messages are actually opened. That's because the websites deliberately send them to people who have just logged on for a trial membership or who have entered their details without committing to any sort of membership. To open their message, they need to become a member and/or upgrade their membership. The websites are using existing customers to bring in new business and they certainly don't have your own interests at heart. Very few ladies will receive your romantic proposition and those that do will be most

upset when they realise they've just coughed up to get a message from someone looking like Keith Richards' grandad.

- Latest Southern hot-spots for single 'on-liners' appear to be Cardiff, Southampton, Bristol, Chelmsford, & Newport.

Please can I apologise for the excessive overuse of the word 'shoes' in the past couple of chapters.

TAKE ON BOARD: United Nations peacekeepers. Ideally, the 'Gay Pride' brigade, whistles and all.

CHAPTER 11: ARE YOU STILL PAYING ATTENTION?

So, what else have we learnt.......

WOMEN LIKE A BIT OF ROUGH: During the 1990's, Martians and Venusians took it upon themselves to meet halfway. They (as in Venusians) decided that as we (sorry, YOU) hadn't managed to understand their own need to change the bedsheets, eat on time, watch soap-operas, phone people just to say hello & recycle, they would try and understand the most basic needs of man. Which is why - when the big match is showing on the 48" plasma screen at your local - the sweaty, belligerent and hairy crowd will be infiltrated by girlies. Wearing footy tops and drinking pints. The Venusian race, with ample time on their pretty little hands, have taken it upon themselves to cross the divide and venture into the previously male-dominated arena of football and beer. As previously stated, the Venusians have long since sussed out what makes us tick. It ain't rocket-science. But despite knowing that man is partly to blame for our inability to co-exist on Planet

Earth 2006AD, the women in our lives have held out their olive branches and pulled themselves into that other little world in which 21st Century man often cocoons himself. That little planet where we go that enables us to escape from the very planet on which we exist - our own little moon. So, they've humoured us, they've shouted, they've tutted and they've gone back to their mothers. Like we're gonna follow! C'mon girls, if you really want us to drop our emotional guard and come after you with open arms and some of those flowers we buy at the local garage everytime we have to say sorry, we're hardly going to follow you there. It's the ultimate in womanly 'hard to get' and is akin to leaping into a vat of nitric acid. But the point is, this is what <u>they</u> (sorry girls, Martian ramble in progress) are programmed to do. But they continue to share our airspace because just like their foremothers before them, they know what we are like. We are reliably and undeniably predictable. So, having humoured us, they've delved into our world to see what makes us tick and unfortunately, many of them have to decided to stay. But at the same time this revolution started to commence, men were attempting their own role reversal and taking on the mantle of 'new man'. Somebody who changed nappies, somebody who stayed at home whilst their other half worked, somebody who cooked and did the housework. By all means, have a delve into this murky world of womanhood but virtually every Martian who dared to venture into this Venusian world, soon jumped back out again. We are pre-programmed. It was while you were doing the dishes and changing the Hoover bag that she was donning her footy top and looking at the Sky fixtures. Women want their men to be masculine and as previously stated, still enjoy being clubbed with the occasional cudgel (figuratively speaking). Those women who still retain the mantle of 'homekeeper', enjoy the reliance that is placed on their cliched hubby in the role of chief wage-earner and/or hunter-gatherer. And those more successful women out there still enjoy the company of a pre-programmed Neanderthal because their man is quite often the only thing they can't control and having a destabilising element in their life, adds spice. Man will never understand woman because only a woman could begin to explain their needs, their views, their moods, their shoes (sorry) but as I've already explained, we are not programmed to listen. And man can't tell man because he doesn't know. So, lets go back to the great divide. Women like a bit of rough, so, - stay unshaven, fart, go to the pub, watch footy, disagree, work late, scratch your balls, drive dangerously, wipe it on the curtains, fancy your neighbour, enjoy politics, belch and believe that you are always right. *Women try to do these things but only because they feel they have to, rather than because they want to. We have had a taste of womanly things (I can feel a rude joke coming on but this late in the book, I will suppress myself) and when the woman in your life beckons you into her world - her own little moon that she exists on whilst resident on Planet Earth - by all means go there. We must continue to share and I urge all guys to actively participate in her little existence and although some of her alien traits - glossy magazines, vegetarian cooking, bingo, 'East-bloody-Enders', laundry, shoes, being fat etc - will be difficult to comprehend, take the time to understand this alien world but <u>only</u> when invited. The line in the sand must be re-drawn. It is bad enough

that the Venusian race has a greater understanding of the Martian mind than vice versa. But its even worse when she comes down the pub with you to watch the game, meaning you have to microwave your own tea when you get back. <u>We are meant to be different!</u>
*If you find that the woman in your life does tend to scratch her balls, I think you're with the wrong person.
BE A CAVEMAN!

The following is a typical profile description from an on-line Venusian, September 2006AD.

"have changed this bit 2nite in the hope of it bein more understandable. lets get the 'i dont want' bits out the way first to save yr time and mine.number 1..To all u 20 somethings I am not 'Mrs Jones'- i probably know yr mother and bitch slappin over someones son isn't on my agenda.(thanks anyway) B...Apparently half the foreign men on ere that speak rubbish english have been waitin for me all their lives and will treat me like a princess,again, thanks but no thanks.number 3...If i wanted 2talk about sex all day i'd talk to my 'rabbit' frankly, he would appear to be far better at it than u lot (u know who u r)And finally D... those wit pics only please and u Players have no place on this or any other site apart from nastyrus.com. Ok,now for both of u that r left lol as u can see i speak my mind, ive been hurt and its not happening again.Due to my job i live in a mans world,which is fine by me as i find the whole 'girlie' thing a bit tricky at times (i do however know how to do the lady thing wen its required).If u wanna go watch the match at wkends thats fine cuz i'll be off watchin mine (proud villa fan)and if u call 2say you'll be late cuz the lads just got another round in,thats fine

too cuz i'll prob be in same situation (even prouder stella
fan)yes, im a strong woman and i'm prob set in my ways
a bit but underneath it all i'm soft as sh** and just lookin
for someone to be my best mate,my lover,my critic, just my
'everythin'. i also believe in bein comfortable with saying
the 'look' of a person is important, so, the 'look' that floats
my boat is that of wot i'd call a geezer, a rough diamond,
a bit of a lad, ya know the type..shaved/very short hair and
broad shoulders, tattoos very welcome. if this helps at all,
ive been told i have an unhealthy fixation wit the likes of
grant mitchell.his looks and sense of humour of chris moyles
would be perfect! anyway, there it is for the world to see,
me and wot i want/dont want".
'NO PLAYERS PLEASE' from Swindon

THERE IS NO HAPPY EVER AFTER: One of the most important things to take out of this book apart from the bookmark and that bit of Pitta bread that fell out of your mouth as you turned the pages, is the fact that there is no 'Happy Ever After'. Ladies, it's all well and good being encamped inside a warm bubble of romance, love and affection with the optimistic outlook that "one day my prince will come" (I'll let you do the jokes, the ammunition being Charles, Camilla and a polo pony), but 'Happy Ever After' just does not exist. 'Happy Ever After' was a 70's sitcom starring Terry Scott. He's dead. Happy Ever After is what happens when the knight in shining armour releases the damsel in distress from a life of solitude and celibacy in the tallest tower of the remotest castle. But this was in his own purely selfish interests. Once he'd straddled her across King Arthur's round-table and lanced her a lot, the chase was over. With dragons to fight, kings to overthrow, armour to polish and more damsels to liberate, he'd be gone quicker than he had come. And that was probably plenty quick enough. Happy Ever After is what usually happens at the end of the greatest love stories ever put on celluloid.

(If any film buffs are reading, yes, celluloid is no longer the format used for movie production and even the classic, digitally-remastered films are now only available on disc format but if you've spent your life remembering such Earth-shattering snippets of info as: Who played Chewbacca in the 'Star Wars' movies and how many extras there were in 'Gandhi', then you've clearly never had sex. With anybody else).

But, thats the end of the film - not the story. When Richard Gere carries Debra Winger out of that factory at the end of 'An Officer and a Gentleman', what Venusians see through their ripped tissue and melting mascara is a Happy Ever After. But what they fail to realise is that Mr.Gere becomes her pimp, smacks his bitch up and tortures her by making her sit through re-runs of all his old movies. In films and books, life stops when we want it to. In real life, we have to see things through to the bitter end. For those of you seeking your perfect 'soulmate', you won't know whether you've found him/her until the day you leave this mortal coil - the person who sits beside your hospital bed in your apres-jiggy days, <u>will</u> be your soulmate. And thats unlikely to be the person you're with now. Love and desperation grows stronger as we get older - just ask anybody who's ever been married on 3 or 4 occasions (or 8 in Elizabeth Taylor's case) and they will always tell you that their most recent husband/wife is/was the best. Anybody who walks up the aisle with somebody who's been married 7 times before must be totally barking, so if they turn out to be the best spouse ever, what does that say about the misguided perception of love that their multi-married partner retains? No, the only films that end with peeps in eternal love are the ones where somebody dies and that, according to 'chick-flick' theory, isn't a Happy Ever After. So, if you really love the one you're with, you could always put a little something extra in their tea to ensure they will forever remain in your heart.

BURY THE HATCHET!

KEEPING IT HOT: In Chapter 3, I highlighted some of the 'chestnuts' that continue to raise their ugly heads on dating websites. These are fairly generic and at least one of these strange alien customs can be found in the DNA of every Venusian: She likes spontaneity, a good sense of humour, tall/dark/handsome zzzzzz, a glass of red wine and men in uniform. She's romantic, impatient, lies about her weight and is currently getting into the gym. And of course, she's a shoe-loving water-babe. But its the water-babe element that is relevant here. As previously stated, on Planet Venus, water didn't/doesn't exist. But whilst resident there, the Venusians yearned for companionship & escapism and they looked upon the invasion by the penile sector as the dawn of a new age. Harmony, peace and understanding would be the new black and lesbianism would forever be eradicated (gutted). But the reason these thoughts were harboured is because the Venusian mind was far inferior to that of the Martian one. But during the 2000+ years since, women have discovered the benefits of water and no longer have the intense heat of Planet Venus as an excuse for their dippyness. And whilst their own brainpower has expanded, life in general (work, drugs, alcohol, 'Hollyoaks') has shrunk the male equivalent. So, it is time to heat things up and slow down their rational thought mechanism. And you thought I was joking in Chapter 3! There are about a dozen countries that straddle the line of the Equator and these are generally regarded as some of the hottest places on Earth. These include the likes of Brazil, the largely unheard of Kiribati (formerly known as the Gilbert Islands) and the aptly named Equatorial Guinea, although the latter doesn't actually lie immediately on the Equator. Other countries include Indonesia, drug-ridden Colombia and the war-torn African nations of Congo & Somalia. It is safe to say that drugs, crime, poverty, religion and civil war play an active part in all countries that have the misfortune to exist on this melting circumference but their peoples co-exist - man and woman - better than the richer, cooler Western world. So, there you have it. Don't expect me to give you the answer to this one. I've done my bit. Turn up the central heating, get a water meter installed, emigrate to a hotter country (although those listed above are probably best avoided), move to the beach, microwave her head every morning. It's up to you but we do need to ensure that her thought process is hindered because the absorption of water into her body - and 70% of everybodys body is water which means she's holding the equivalent of 14 stone - is partly to blame for the situation we find ourselves in nowadays. Stop laughing, it's true!

HAVE THE TAP DRIPPING BUT NEVER FULL ON.

"well here goes, what can i say,good sometimes wicked sense of humour, can be a stroppy cow too but can't we all if we are honest!! Not looking for a one night stand with some loser that cant hold down a relationship, and i'm not interested in large ego's that need to be massaged, If your're interested say so, don't B.S.I'm looking for the w package and yes i believe in the happy ever after fairytale, just never found it yet.Don't want a guy with a large wallet just a large heart!and don't want to be anyones F**K buddy! The pic shows my hair as long and dark.... not so anymore it is now in a bob with blonde streaks. the rest is just the same though. I go to the gym 5 times a week to try and fight time!! Had no nips, tucks, sucks or implants ...Yet so it's all real.I am not perfect and don't pretent to be, what you see is what you get, I'm told by nearly everyone that i have gorgeous eyes (you will have to judge for yourself)I'm 5ft7" and a size 14 but shrinking rapidly due to the gym, Love all the girlie things like having my nails done and buying clothes. I love romance and cuddles, I am loyal and caring (sound like a labrador here) I don't bite unless asked nicely!!! LOL looking to spend the rest of my life with a man who blows my mind daily and in return i will do the same for him.Only guys with a picture will get a reply, if a dimwit like me can manage to get a pic on here so can you!!! good luck to you all and hope you find the perfect person for you Xx Ally One last thing if you know the song these are the first words to you could be the one for me.. fav song ever and no clues for you!!! "And i would give up forever to touch you, coz i know that you feel me somehow, your the closest to heaven that i'll ever be and I don't wanna go home right now.And all i can taste is this moment and all i can breathe is your life and sooner or

later it's over i just don't wanna miss you tonight, Best song in the world.. from a great film!!!"

TAKE ON BOARD - Homer Simpson. "They are ravenous, bloodsucking monsters. Compliment them and they want more, more, MORE. But it's always worth it in the end!"

CHAPTER 12: HITTING THE RIGHT BUTTONS

It's now 1 year since I commenced this book. When I started writing, I harboured fears for the future of mankind. Of course, some Venusians amongst you would say that the words 'man' and 'kind' should never feature in the same sentence. So, for ultimate unification amid this closing chapter, we'll call it people-kind. Things haven't changed much in 12 months and man & woman appear to be as hellbent as ever on destroying any future our children and grandchildren have of creating a mutually harmonious existence. The purpose of my book was to emphasise the obvious shortfalls both sexes have but rather than analyse the data in a psychological way and record my findings in a best-seller only read by eggheads, I have made it accessible to both sets of beings. Like a good catheter, I have generally taken the piss but you will have felt the benefit. I am neither a psychologist, comedian or writer. But what I am is a person who understands what it is to be in a loving relationship and a sexual relationship, although not necessarily at the same time. Many of the facts and data

I've submitted during the preceeding chapters won't be new to you but its only by my stating the obvious to those of you currently blinded by your own perceptions of what love and communication is all about, will you truly understand the dire straits we are currently in and the horrific inevitability of its consequences. It is Apocalypse Now. Some of the greatest writers ever to have put pen or quill to paper were those who took an absolutely outside perspective of the world they were writing about. Of course, this is an inevitable consequence because literature is a time-consuming labour of solitude. To write about Victorian London to the extent that Dickens did, required the ability to live it, breathe it, understand it but ultimately, be detached from it. I am more dick-head than Dickens but I too have sacrificed the world I want to be within, to enable my readers to get there too. I was also hoping that writing this book may actually improve my love-life. Wrong. Ultimately, what I have tried to do here is build 2 ships: a theoretical spaceship that will take my readers of the male gender back to the promised land, where understanding and communicating with the non-male species becomes almost second-nature. And the literal spaceship, which we may have to use to pursue our better halves across the cosmos - or at least head them off at the pass (and no, that isn't an obscure sexual term) - should they decide to return to their planet of origin. Of course, the whole business of building a 'literal' spaceship is extremely relevant because as Planet Earth continues to become more inhabitable by the day, a search for pastures new is almost inevitable. And a mutual one at that.

CASEBOOK NO.5: Casebook No.5 took place in August 2005, shortly after my previous encounters but far too late for inclusion within the early drafts of this book. Kim was/is from Newport and sounded much as I imagined she would. Very Welsh. Now, Newport in Rhode Island U.S.A would've been cool. Newport in the Isle Of Wight would've been less enchanting but far more accessible and would've given me the opportunity to tell my I.O.W joke:

What's long, brown and steaming and comes out of cows? Answer: The Isle Of Wight ferry. But its not so I won't.

No, this was Newport in Gwent, a place that spawned 'Goldie Lookin' Chain' and (allegedly) has the highest arson rate in Europe. Lush. So, on a bright summery day in Cheltenham, I was paid a visit by a lovely 33(ish)yr-old from Wales and we enjoyed a scoff and a glass of wine alfresco style in the town centre. Kim later told me that her home town couldn't offer such cosmopolitan outside eateries although judging by what I've heard of the town, eating outside is all some of their firebomb victims can do! My only vague memory of our 'brief encounter' was the fact that she wore green shoes. Until recently, Kim & I kept in touch on a regular basis but having cancelled or deferred numerous opportunities for us to reunite, I felt that her heart wasn't really in it. I've since discovered that women have feigned their own death to avoid actually meeting me, preferring to keep our relationship long-distant, so making a potential cross-contamination of the species nigh on impossible. Maybe we'll stay as long-distant friends but without 100% input from myself, I know that is unlikely to happen. Kim & I have since lost touch, hence her inclusion in my book. A lovely girl and I wish her well.

CASEBOOK NO.6: One year on and once again, I'm surfing for potential mates amongst the multitude of websites that cater for one-armed bandits such as me. If u wanna talk dirty and show your genitals, there's a site for you. If u wanna talk to fellow parents (talk bout kids? Yeah right!), there's a site for you. If you want good old fashioned romance, there's a site too. One of the many ladies who responded to my mating call was a lass from Stratford-Upon-Avon, who shall remain anonymous. She gives me e-mail address - I send my life story - she replies with cryptic one-liner - I send more info bout me - she replies with cryptic on-liner yet again. Hmmm. Her e-mails were along the lines of "mail me again happy head" & "you sound gorgeous". Although she had summed me up pretty accurately, I knew little of this much-travelled, 39yr-old Greek-sounding lady, who looked scarily like my X (see Chapter 3). She described her interests as "picnics, folk festivals, modern boating and manners". OK, so the warning signs were there but as I've previously stated, opposites do attract and this shouldn't put off potential suitors. We are from completely different planets for Christs sake, so what d'ya expect? So, I rang her as requested and expecting a sultry, squeaky voice, found myself talking to Deirdre Barlow. As we chatted, I could picture the tendons straining in her neck and those great big f**k off glasses that she wears astride her miserable face. Maybe this is what all 39yr-olds sound like on the phone. Whereas 12yr-old boys suddenly go from soprano to tenor-bass on the drop of a testicle, the throat of a woman goes from being silky smooth to being as rough as a moggys tongue over a 12yr period, *12yrs being the average length of a marriage before the inevitable. Aided by years of smoking, red wine and continuous bellowing at previous partners, she now has a hoarse voice to accompany her horse face. Anyway, I proceeded to chat to Deidre and this "bubbly, leggy blonde" who enjoyed "not acting her age" told me about her fiancee who had committed suicide 6yrs previous. Very sad and she'd obviously been through a lot but was this the same person who had graced the screen of my monitor just days before? Then I asked her what 'modern boating' is. "Whats that?" Deirde replied. Alarm bells rang and so ended our one and only conversation. I asked for more info and pics via e-mail but received nothing. She left messages on my answerphone and got ditto. She could be a fork-lift truck driver called Trevor for all I know and its that element of mystery that many peeps find so attractive about the perils of on-line dating. Scary but true.

(*I actually made this figure up but it sounds about right and if it wasn't for the fact that I am owning up to this little misdemeanour, you - the reader - would be none the wiser).

CASEBOOK NO.7: My final casebook and although this friendship is in its infancy, this could yet be the happy ever after (OK, I know, there is no H.E.A) that I mentioned in Chapter 5. I started communicating with a certain lady from up north in early-August 2006 and at the time of writing, we've already spent a w/e together and there's a fair chance we will meet again. I think that's all you need to know.

"Next time you are frustrated with the opposite sex, remember men are from Mars and women are from Venus. Even if you don't remember anything else from this book, remembering that we are supposed to be different will help you to be more

*loving. By gradually releasing your judgements and blame
and persistently asking for what you want, you can create the
loving relationships you want, need and deserve. You have
a lot to look forward to. May you continue to grow in love
and light. Thank-you for letting me make a difference in your
life". JOHN GRAY Ph.D*

.....and hopefully, I have too. Because we have addressed some
of the problems that face both sexes on this ever diminishing
planet and I believe I have equipped you physically and
mentally, for some of the tough battles ahead. Even if we do
have to flee further afield to continue to co-exist, you will
have the necessary tools on board: your La-Z-boy chair, a
map, a pair of handcuffs, walkie-talkies, copious amounts of
strong lager, a barristers wig, Homer Simpson, a lie-detector,
a toolbox, copies of 'National Geographic', some Coronation
Chicken sarnies, United Nations peacekeepers and most
importantly of all, Angeline Jolie and a copy of this book.
What else could you possibly need? Well come to think
about it, "women are desirable, enigmatic, ambitious, sexy
and - let's face it boys - as downright unfathomable as ever".
So, I've barely touched the surface...........

Do Eskimos put ice in their drinks?

Apparently not. But its not because they have too
much ice already. Many Eskimo's or people of the Inuit do
indeed still rely on their icy surroundings for their water.
The water is melted via boiling, a process which also
eliminates any impurities, thus making it drinkable. But
in townships and other uniglooised (as in un-igloo-ised....a
word I just invented) communities, water is brought in via
a heated water tanker. Natural water supplies via pipes is

impossible because of the elements. But these communities also receive supplies of well-known soft drinks and other alternatives to water and as these are often brought in at a higher temperature which us Westerners would find uncomfortable to drink, ice - as a cooling medium - would appear to be an ideal accompaniment. But ice in its purest form is not normally deemed to be digestable for one major reason.....moose piss. Enough said.

Whatever happened to white dog crap?

There are 2 conflicting arguments as to why white dog poo has disappeared off our pavements over the past couple of decades, both of which seem to be believable, if not entirely watertight. Growing up in the 1970's, white dog poo seemed to put in more appearances than flared trousers and Jimmy Saville. But in those days, we had a thing called a 'butchers' which was a local, friendly store that sold fresh meat and where senior citizens could get chatted up and their dogs could get fed for nothing. Dogs were fed bones and by eating half a ton of raw calcium, their turds turned white and lay like sticks of chalk upon the kerbside. Forward to the 21st Century and dogs are fed tins of reconstituted, smelly, brown muck....then we wonder why their turds look and smell so bad!

The other argument is that in 'those' days, dog poo was more acceptable and it wasn't illegal to have your pooch pooing in the street, hence it lay around longer and naturally dried in the sun. So turning white. Sounds complete crap to me.

Thank-you for having me, or not as the case proved to be.
PHIL COOK

Printed in the United Kingdom
by Lightning Source UK Ltd.
128140UK00001B/34-42/A